Policy in Criminal Justice
Current Perspectives from InfoTrac

Michael Fischer

Norfolk State University

WADSWORTH
CENGAGE Learning

Australia • Brazil • Japan • Korea • Mexico • Singapore • Spain • United Kingdom • United States

WADSWORTH
CENGAGE Learning

For product information and technology assistance, contact us at **Cengage Learning Customer & Sales Support, 1-800-354-9706**

For permission to use material from this text or product, submit all requests online at **www.cengage.com/permissions** Further permissions questions can be emailed to **permissionrequest@cengage.com**

ISBN-13: 978-1-439-03672-3
ISBN-10: 1-439-03672-1

Cover Image: © Jeff Spielman / Getty Images

Wadsworth
10 Davis Drive
Belmont, CA 94002-3098
USA

Cengage Learning is a leading provider of customized learning solutions with office locations around the globe, including Singapore, the United Kingdom, Australia, Mexico, Brazil, and Japan. Locate your local office at: **www.cengage.com/global**

Cengage Learning products are represented in Canada by Nelson Education, Ltd.

To learn more about Brooks/Cole, visit **www.cengage.com/wadsworth**

Purchase any of our products at your local college store or at our preferred online store **www.ichapters.com**

Printed in the United States of America
1 2 3 4 5 6 7 13 12 11 10 09

Contents

Preface

Criminal Justice Policy

"The degree of civilization can be judged by entering its prisons," said Dostoevsky. Some conservatives have countered that to judge how society treats its disadvantaged should instead be measured by how effectively it protects innocents from offenders. Civil libertarians stress legal procedures to assure equity and fairness in the hope that such procedures will maximize substantive rights. Construction of law, orientations of policing, and incarceration policy reflect our conception of justice. Concern for just and effective criminal justice administration obviously involves a number of complex issues. This collection of articles addresses historical approaches and cutting-edge innovations in criminal justice policy. The five topic areas, i.e., Fixing Broken Windows and Community Policing, White Collar Crime, Specialty Courts, Incarcerated Women and their Children, and Serious Juvenile Offenders reflect current ideas of leading professionals from a range of careers in criminal justice.

Topic one highlights Chief William Bratton's Crime Control Model in both New York and Los Angeles. It encompasses Fixing Broken Windows Theory, Zero Tolerance Policing, COMSTAT, Organizational Development Management, and coordinated criminal justice/non criminal justice agency planning and program implementation to reduce crime and disorder. Community policing policies are presented as an alternative to Fixing Broken Windows theory. These policies entail problem solving without aggressive arrest-focused strategies. Police can actively work with government and non-governmental agencies to find alternatives to incarceration for delinquent youth, the mentally ill, and single mothers who commit non-violent offenses. Critics of Zero Tolerance Policy, therefore, assert that to police as though people matter means finding them homeless shelters, not arresting them for public order offenses.

Topic two addresses elite white-collar crime. Crimes against consumers, unsafe products, environmental crime, securities, corporate and fiduciary fraud, insider trading, embezzlement, etc., cause more economic loss and bodily injury and greater erosion of public confidence than does street crime. Recent revelations about scandals on Wall Street, in the banking industry, and in government have raised collective awareness of the threat to our society of elite white-collar crime. Articles in this section address the lure of white-collar crime as well as proposed sentencing reform.

Topic three examines judicial justice by looking at specialty courts. Since 1989 when the first American drug court was established in Miami, more than 2300 of these courts have become operational. Whereas traditional drug rehabilitation programs have been ineffective, drug courts, which include court monitored wrap-around, long-term treatment and supervision have shown markedly improved success rates. Mental health courts also use the power of the court to monitor treatment for non-violent mentally ill offenders, who participate in supervised long-term treatment in place of incarceration. Specialty courts thus have contributed to improved justice.

Attachment theorists have long asserted that a secure infant-parent bond is essential for the development of a productive, healthy, and moral individual. Topic four involves the consequences of separating female offenders and their children. The dramatic increase in female incarceration, from about 10,000 in prison and jail in the early 1970s to about 225,000 today, is cause for alarm for any concerned American citizen. What is this doing to the children of these mothers, one-sixth of whom deliver while in jail or prison or give birth in the year before incarceration? This topic addresses strategies that the criminal justice system can adopt to help these children and their incarcerated mothers. However, this collection does not explore how to reverse the social conditions or criminal justice policies that led to such an unprecedented increase in female confinement. Nevertheless, it is certainly worthy of pursuit for scholars, researchers, and practitioners.

Topic five involves serious juvenile offenders. The objective of the Child Savers of the 19th century was to use the power of the state to act in the best interest of the child. It was assumed that youth have the potential to become moral and autonomous citizens and that the well-ordered society can guide delinquents' redemption through paternalistic intervention. Fair principles of justice demand that youth who lack reason, experience, and understanding should have their liberty rights protected while learning how to conform to society's norms. However, the due process approach of the 1960s followed by a get-tough approach since the 1980s have led to the adoption of punishment as a legitimate objective for juvenile offenders. Stress is placed upon rules of procedure in an adversarial process that can mete out long and harsh sentences. Articles for this last topic argue that such practice is unjust and is based on an unrealistic understanding of developmental criminology and delinquent trajectories. On the other hand, theory and data are presented to support the position that a certain percentage of anti-social youth may be beyond the reach of rehabilitation and will continue to pose a serious threat to citizen safety. Whether young offenders are perceived as deserving punishment or not, there is agreement that primary prevention programs put in place early can minimize the development of serious delinquency.

This collection of articles presents a variety of cutting-edge viewpoints on critical issues in criminal justice. The strategies police adopt as gatekeepers of the criminal justice system, the growing awareness of the nature and scope of elite white-collar crime, drug and mental health specialty courts, the rapidly increasing incarceration of women, and the current orientation of juvenile court, are central issues in criminal justice. Understanding these topics prepares one to make informed decisions about criminal justice policy.

Part 1

Fixing Broken Windows and Community Policing

1

How to Win the War Against Crime

William J. Bratton

Since I became commissioner in 1994, the New York Police Department has been engaged in a full-scale attack on crime. Reported crime continued to decline in the first quarter of 1996 -- 33 percent since 1993. Homicides are down 49 percent.

But even before I and several senior staff members resigned, the media and the public had been wondering how long these trends could continue. Their skepticism is understandable, but I believe there is still room for significant reductions. When I became the Transit Police chief in 1990, no one predicted that subway robberies would decline by 76 percent in the next six years, but it happened. The techniques that turned the Transit Police around have been used to re-engineer the N.Y.P.D.

The department's goal for 1996 is to reduce crime by 10 percent. Five steps need to be continued to achieve it.

Empower the precinct commanders. This was probably the most important reform we made. We gave these front-line managers the authority to run their precincts as miniature police departments without a lot of petty interference from headquarters. The best ones rose to this opportunity with enthusiasm and creativity. We should continue to empower them.

Insure accountability. We developed a process called CompStat, to insure that our commanders received strategic guidance. CompStat is a system of accountability that uses computerized crime statistics, electronic pin mapping and intensive strategy sessions, during which the highest ranking managers of the N.Y.P.D. quiz precinct commanders about crime problems. CompStat is essential for further success.

How to Win the War Against Crime, by William J. Bratton (1996). The New York Times, April 5, 1996. Copyright © 1996 The New York Times. Reprinted by permission.

4

Address quality-of-life offenses. There is no such thing as a minor crime in the sense that lesser offenses create an atmosphere of fear and disorder that sets the stage for major crimes. We have moved against low-level drug dealers, street prostitutes, boom-box cars, squeegee pests and other violators. The department shouldn't slip back into the old view that such offenses are a low priority.

Attack crime strategically. Today's department doesn't just try to solve individual crimes. We counter crime patterns and dismantle criminal enterprises. Detectives interrogate everyone arrested -- even people arrested for minor crimes -- to gather the best intelligence about other crimes and crime patterns. We focus on the fences who help burglars, the chop shops and exporters who serve auto thieves and the gun dealers who supply drug gangs and armed robbers. We have concentrated on the city's trouble spots, cutting handgun homicides by 40 percent in two years.

This tactic takes coordination among patrol officers, detectives and narcotics officers, which was largely unheard of in the old days. In the past, many of the department's specialized squads worked 9 to 5, while our competition, the criminals, worked 24 hours a day, seven days a week. No wonder they were winning.

Reward cops. The N.Y.P.D., with 38,000 officers, has had sufficient personnel to attack crime. But officers are increasingly restive about their stagnant wages, reduced overtime, worsening working conditions and declining numbers. These issues must be addressed.

This past week, the department initiated the largest, most comprehensive antidrug initiative ever undertaken by an urban police department. Its goal is to permanently eradicate drug sales in northern Brooklyn, which account for about 20 percent of the city's homicides and shootings. The initiative will help the department achieve its goal of a double-digit decline in crime in 1996.

But the efforts of the police alone are not enough. The continued support of Mayor Rudolph Giuliani, the public and the criminal justice system will be vital. I am confident that the Mayor and his next Police Commissioner, Howard Safir, who has a broad law enforcement background, will build on the successes of the past six years.

4

2

Focus on Community Policing

Fostering Community Partnerships that Prevent Crime and Promote Quality of Life

Clyde L. Cronkhite

During the past decade, crime has decreased in urban areas, but, subsequently, some rural communities have experienced an increase because offenders have been forced away from large cities. This trend threatens the quality of life in many suburban and rural areas. Therefore, a growing number of townships are taking a proactive posture against this movement by focusing on community-based crime prevention programs, which unite communities in the fight to thwart the spread of crime.

THE CHALLENGE

McDonough County, Illinois, is in the western part of the state with a population of approximately 40,000 and includes Macomb, a university town of 20,000 residents plus 12,000 college students. Although Macomb offers a family friendly atmosphere with a low crime rate, harbingers of gang and drug activities surfaced, perhaps from an influx of individuals seeking a haven from the increased law enforcement efforts in larger cities. Drug arrests began to occur and evidence of graffiti appeared. Therefore, citizens of Macomb decided to handle these problems by drawing from their community-based, crime prevention program experiences. Macomb's results may serve as a model for other cities confronting similar trends.

Focus on community policing: Fostering community partnerships that prevent crime and promote quality of life, by Clyde Cronkhite (2005). The FBI Law Enforcement Bulletin, May 2005, v74 i5 p7 (4). Used by permission of FBI Law Enforcement Bulletin and Clyde Cronkhite. Endnotes have been deleted.

THE CONCEPT

Many of today's crime prevention approaches are based on an experiment conducted in a New Jersey community years ago, which spotlighted the importance of maintaining neighborhoods to keep communities relatively crime free. The broken windows theory holds that such issues as street maintenance and lighting, limits on the number of families living in a single dwelling, and control of absentee landlord rentals reduce crime. Additionally, attention to minor infractions that erode well-kept, safe environments, such as loud music, abandoned cars, and graffiti, can prevent the spread of gang violence, drug abuse, and other criminal conduct. Macomb applied the broken windows concept in a rural environment by forming community partnerships that result in a continuous focus on quality-of-life issues.

THE APPROACH

In early 1994, Macomb formed a Crime and Quality of Life Advisory Committee, changing the name in 1996 to Community Quality of Life Committee and expanding the purview to include all of McDonough County. The committee seeks "to support efforts that contribute to the excellence of our community and to monitor and give advice regarding maintaining and enhancing community quality of life, including the prevention and reduction of crimes that adversely impact our neighborhoods."

The committee recruited concerned citizens who have a responsibility for quality of life and criminal justice academicians from the local university, as well as other community leaders. Several committee members, such as the fire chief, sheriff, mayor, school superintendent, executive director of the housing authority, and the local state senator, were selected because their positions have the responsibility and authority to provide a prospering neighborhood.

The major responsibility of the advisory committee involves developing a method for measuring the quality of life in the community, setting a baseline, and monitoring its status. To complete this task, a criminal justice research specialist (a member of the committee) and graduate assistants from the local university's department of law enforcement and justice administration analyzed 26 years of crime trends in Macomb and McDonough County, comparing them with eight contiguous counties and totals for the state of Illinois. They selected "community wellness" indicators (e.g., poverty and welfare rates, per capita income, single parent families, births by mothers under 18 years of age, truancy violations, and emergency room admissions) from their research.

The committee meets at least four times a year, and members review these indicators. Then, they publish a community "report card" or "wellness report." Any indication that the community is adversely affected requires recommendations for combating the negative factors before they become substantial problems.

As a result of the crime trend analysis, committee members noted early signs of substance abuse and gang involvement in the crime trends. As a result, the committee formed a youth task force that meets monthly. The task force determines the extent of the problem, confirms what is being done about the issue, recognizes any unnecessary duplication of services, decides the need for additional action and what it should be, and recommends steps that advisory committee members should take.

The school superintendent and a local religious leader oversee the youth task force. Several of the advisory committee members, such as the police chief and director of the housing authority, serve on the task force as well. Additionally, persons who deal daily with youth problems comprise part of the task force, along with an individual from the university who is an expert in substance abuse problems.

Task force members have made several recommendations, such as school dress codes, truancy enforcement, a youth teen center, and ordinances to restrict alcohol and tobacco use by minors to combat the growing crime trend. At the youth center, teens socialize in a nonalcoholic environment and participate in an annual film festival. Also, the task force uses the local cable television channel and area newspapers to alert parents about gangs and substance abuse among teens.

Task force members collected information about nearly 100 community activities available to youths and conveyed it to parents and teens through the local media and a Web site. They also made the information available to practitioners who deal with young people in trouble. Members encouraged police officers to divert underage offenders to these community activities, rather than counseling and releasing them.

Additionally, when rental property inhabited by students around the local university began to deteriorate, the task force recommended an adopt-a-street program, which made various university student organizations responsible for preserving quality of life in their own neighborhoods. This program, implemented throughout the police department, has proven successful.

RECOGNITION DAYS

The advisory committee recommended spotlighting people who and activities that enhance well-maintained communities. This evolved into a yearly event held each September and includes exhibits and demonstrations by most county public safety agencies. Local schools bring students to the event where thousands of community members meet police, fire, emergency, and rescue officers. Community members have the opportunity to thank these public employees and have their pictures taken with them, pet the police dogs, climb the fire equipment, sound the police siren, and perform other such activities. The celebration includes a supplement in the local newspaper that commends and provides photographs of members of the county public safety agencies. The committee gives awards to individual agencies, as well as to citizens who contribute to a safe community. This yearly event fosters communication and trust between the public safety agencies and the community and promotes awareness of the relationship between public safety and community quality of life. During the past 10 years, nearly 100 citizens and organizations have been honored for their contributions to local quality of life.

CONCLUSION

As crime, particularly drug use and gang violence, seeps into smaller communities, some townships are implementing procedures to deter its spreading. The crime prevention and quality-of-life effort in McDonough County, Illinois, seeks to prevent this ever-increasing threat. An advisory committee oversees the program and promotes cooperation and coordination among the various entities that have a responsibility for ensuring a flourishing community.

The committee established and continually monitors community wellness indicators. When these indicators disclose the beginning signs of activities that adversely will impact quality of life, committee members create task forces to recommend remedies.

Then, these solutions are implemented through the committee and aim to prevent community infections before they become serious.

When this project began in the early 1990s, crime had begun its downward trend across the country. However, in Macomb, Illinois, as in many smaller communities, crime was on the rise. After the implementation of this program, crime has decreased and quality of life has become a hallmark of the community.

Anyone involved in resolving social problems realizes that no perfect solutions exist. However, insightful, preventative activities can inhibit and even preclude many adverse conditions that result in the deterioration of community quality of life and the increase of crime. The approach taken by McDonough County may serve as a useful model to other localities working to prevent crime and preserve a nurturing community.

Dr. Cronkhite, a former police practitioner, is a law enforcement and justice administration professor, commentator, and consultant at Western Illinois University in Macomb.

Part 2

White Collar Crime

1

Fraud Inc.

Crime is big business in Florida, generating more money than manufacturing. Medicare fraud alone adds an estimated $12 billion to the state's economy.

David Villano

Like many hardworking immigrants, 39-year-old Eduardo Moreno arrived in south Florida with pennies in his pocket and dreams of striking it rich. By late 2006, the Cuban-born Moreno was running a fast-growing cluster of medical supply companies and clinics and living the good life, with a spacious lake-view home in Miami and a fleet of cars that included a $200,000 Rolls-Royce Phantom.

Moreno and his fortune are both long gone. Investigators say Moreno's businesses amounted mostly to an elaborate scheme to divert millions of dollars in fraudulent Medicare claims into his private bank account. According to a federal indictment, Moreno's companies--Brenda Medical Supply, Faster Medical Supply and RTC of Miami--routinely recruited patients for the sole purpose of billing the government for drug infusion therapies and for medical equipment such as electric wheelchairs, scooters and therapeutic mattresses.

In many cases, officials say, the drugs were unnecessary or never administered and the equipment--including air mattresses costing $868 apiece--was never delivered. More than $7 million in Medicare claims remains under scrutiny.

Fraud Inc: Crime is big business in Florida, generating more money than manufacturing. Medicare fraud alone adds an estimate 12 billion to the state's economy: White collar (2008) crime, by David Villano. Florida Trend, July 2008 v51 i4 p64 (5).

Moreno, arrested a year ago on multiple fraud charges, isn't around to speak in his own defense. He skipped out on a $450,000 bond and remains a fugitive.

But even if all $7 million in Medicare claims turns out to be spurious, that sizable haul makes Moreno just another bit player amid a host of fraudulent enterprises--healthcare fraud, mortgage fraud, consumer fraud, insurance fraud and other categories of white-collar crime--that collectively amount to one of Florida's biggest industries ("The Value of Florida Fraud" page 66).

Recent headline-making cases include a $194-million hedge fund scheme out of West Palm Beach; a $12-million pump-and-dump securities scam in Fort Lauderdale; $6 million swindled from investors in a bogus anti-aging product in Pompano Beach; and a Fort Lauderdale viatical life insurance scam that netted more than $826 million from thousands of victims.

By itself, Medicare fraud in south Florida adds up to big business. In 2007, for example, 197 people were arrested in south Florida and charged with submitting hundreds of millions of dollars in bogus Medicare claims. In one case, a Miami air-conditioning repairman posed as a pharmacist to bilk the government out of $14 million, claiming he was producing aerosol medications. In another, clinic owners allegedly pocketed $12.5 million in Medicare reimbursements, substituting saline solution for expensive HIV medications.

The prosecuted cases, says R. Alexander Acosta, U.S. Attorney for the Southern District of Florida, are just "the tip of the iceberg."

In many ways, the fraud industry in Florida resembles the state's legitimate business community--highly entrepreneurial, comprising mostly small businesses that collectively add up to a lot of economic activity. While crooked politicians and multimillion-dollar scams grab the headlines, experts say the majority of fraud schemes in Florida are committed by the white-collar equivalent of the petty criminal. "These people are often very entrepreneurial, hardworking, but they've found a way to break the law, and they're not afraid to do it" says Acosta.

Attaching a dollar amount to overall fraudulent activity in the state is tricky. Some experts cite an International Monetary Fund estimate that as much as 5% of the world's GDP is generated through fraudulent business activity. As a percentage of Florida's GDP, that calculation would top $36 billion. The Association of Certified Fraud Examiners cites a similar number--5%, or another $36 billion a year statewide--as the estimated loss in corporate revenue from various forms of occupational fraud: Inventory and payroll theft, skimming, billing schemes.

But while the sums seem large and the cases generate big headlines, fraud in Florida isn't, overall, disproportionate to the state's size. In bank, internet and consumer fraud, for example, the state ranks from second to fourth in the nation--consistent with its population rank.

A more meaningful number may be an estimate of how much money fraud imports into the state. Consider: If a resident of Orlando defrauds a Boca Raton resident in a stock scam, the theft represents no real new net economic activity, rather just a transfer of money legitimately earned in Boca Raton that winds up in the pockets of the crook.

In the case of Medicare fraud, how ever, the money comes from outside the state--from the federal treasury. Assuming the stolen money isn't immediately funneled into offshore accounts, the sums generated by the fraud flow in some degree through Florida's legitimate economy, representing a net economic benefit to the state from crime.

And a look at several kinds of fraud that are particularly prevalent in Florida indicates that it pumps a significant amount of money into the state. Some federal officials estimate as much as 20% of the nation's total Medicare fraud occurs in Florida, importing some $12 billion a year into our economy.

The ill-gotten gains don't end up stuffed in mattresses. Many of today's fraudsters deal in so-called "clean money" in plain view of bank officers and IRS investigators. Most Medicare fraud profits, for example, arrive via government check, are legally banked, invested and declared on income statements. And, of course, they're spent in the broader economy, stimulating sales of luxury goods, real estate and other trappings of the well-heeled. Like Moreno, scam artists "are going out and living the good life," says Acosta. "The analogy of (white-collar criminals) being like the old free-spending cocaine cowboys is pretty much on the mark."

Another sector of fraud from which Florida arguably derives a net economic benefit is money laundering. Despite tightened bank secrecy laws, many experts agree that huge sums are flowing illegally in and out of Florida.

Charles Intriago, a former assistant U.S. prosecutor, founder of Money Laundering Alert newsletter and a leading authority on the economics of white-collar crime, estimates that $25 billion a year is laundered in Florida. The source of those billions is myriad: Drugs, fraud schemes, even terrorism finance. Much of the money, like the billions in bogus Medicare reimbursements, is pumped into our economy from outside the state and ends up fueling sales of condos, exotic cars, fancy restaurants and nightclubs and goods at high-end retail stores.

In addition, Intriago says $1.5 billion in laundered money arrives in Florida each year from corrupt Latin American and Caribbean officials and business operators. He points to two high-profile cases: A colonel working for former Peruvian intelligence chief Vladimiro Montesinos and Byron Jerez, former Nicaraguan tax commissioner, both of whom illegally transferred to Miami millions of dollars pilfered or extorted from government coffers.

"These guys are up here living high on the hog--apartments on Miami Beach, Key Biscayne--and their countrymen back home are starving," Intriago says. "And there are plenty more just like them we'll never know about."

Florida International University finance professor John Zdanowicz says the latest laundering trick is to move money into or out of the U.S. by misstating the value of import or export items. A Miami exporter, for example, might ship $1,000 worth of pencils to Colombia, but the invoice will ask for $100,000 in return. Using a computer program he developed, Zdanowicz calculates that so-called trade-based money laundering in Florida topped $8.2 billion last year.

The cost of fraud to the state? In addition to the funds spent on law enforcement, economists and businesspeople cite other impacts. One national mortgage company pulled out of south Florida because the region was generating a hugely disproportionate share of the fraud cases the company experienced. Meanwhile, Stephen Morrell, a professor of economics and finance at Miami's Barry University and a senior research fellow at Florida TaxWatch is concerned by how scams damage Florida's reputation, which he says hurts legitimate business by discouraging relocations and new investment.

As a business proposition, fraud is likely to remain attractive, even luring criminals from other, riskier endeavors. Acosta explains it as "the rate of return versus the criminal exposure." While a drug offense can lead to 20 years in prison (or perhaps a bullet in the head); a $1-million mortgage fraud conviction can lead to probation and community service.

A correct assumption, says Shanna Van Slyke, a doctoral candidate at the Florida State University College of Criminology, who studies sentencing outcomes of white-collar crimes in Florida. She says judges often ignore sentencing guidelines, sparing non-violent criminals from jail time even when the monetary value of the offense is substantial. Judges are especially lenient, she notes, when the victim is the government (as with Medicare fraud) or a faceless corporation, rather than an individual.

"The public perception is that the risk of going to jail is low," Van Slyke says, "which may be the contributing factor when someone crosses the line between a legal and a illegal business practice."

Col. Vicki L. Cutcliffe, director of the Division of Insurance Fraud at the Florida Department of Financial Services, says schemes are growing in size and sophistication, with organized rings--some foreign-based--increasingly common. Recidivism is up. "As long as the rewards are high and deterrent is low," she says, "these people will be out there, always looking to be one step ahead of us."

And Florida's wealth and entrepreneurial culture will likely keep it fertile ground for fraudsters. "People come here to strike it rich--legitimately or otherwise," says former U.S. Attorney Marcos Jimenez, now a Miami attorney in private practice. "These scam artists realize that Florida is a much easier place to operate and to slip in and out of, than say, Omaha."

Eduardo Moreno lived the good life--until he was arrested on suspicion of Medicare fraud. He skipped out on a $450,000 bond.

RELATED ARTICLE: FRAUD'S WIDE REACH

Florida's fraud schemes are creative and wide ranging. Here are some:

Mortgage Fraud

A federal jury convicted Tampa's Ramzy Moumneh and Kamal Moumneh, along with three codefendants in a complex mortgage fraud scheme targeting homeowners facing foreclosure. Prosecutors say homeowners were tricked into selling their properties to straw buyers, with the promise that the title would be returned after 12 monthly lease payments. Instead, the defendants obtained new mortgage loans in excess of the balance owed on the existing mortgage, siphoning some $2 million in equity.

Insurance Fraud

A federal judge sentenced Jacksonville's Thomas D. King to 14 years in prison for overseeing a massive insurance fraud operation that left thousands of employees in eight states without coverage. As owner of the now-defunct Miralink Group, King pocketed more than $5 million from small-business owners who believed they were paying for workers' compensation and other services.

Bank Fraud

Hector Orlansky, former president of Miami-based E.S. Bankest, was sentenced to 20 years for bank fraud and other charges stemming from the loss of $164 million by Portugal-based Espirito Santo Financial Group. E.S. Bankest was in the business of factoring--buying other companies' receivables at a discount--but prosecutors say Orlansky earned millions by falsifying records to receive collateralized bank loans needed to finance risky acquisitions.

Occupational Fraud

Frederick Bradley Nowetl of Homestead was sentenced to seven years in prison after pleading guilty to a long-running occupational fraud scam at the engineering construction firm where he served as a high-ranking executive. Prosecutors say Nowell, while vice president of the Redland Co., embezzled more than $11 million by approving false vendor payments to companies he owned.

Investment Fraud

A federal jury convicted the last of 12 defendants on investment fraud charges in connection with a $60-million pyramid scheme. Prosecutors say Canadian Jerrold L. Gunn of Niceville promised returns in excess of 360% annually for the purchase of secret U.S. treasury obligations. The investment program was a sham, and new investors' money was used to pay earlier investors.

Business Fraud

Russell G. MacArthur Jr. of Hollywood pleaded guilty to helping dupe investors out of more than $19 million in a business opportunity fraud scheme involving the sale of DVD vending machines. Federal prosecutors say MacArthur and other principals with Hollywood-based American Entertainment Distributors exaggerated potential profits, falsely promised to secure locations for the machines and used phony references to lure prospective purchasers.

Medicaid Fraud

A jury convicted a Miami dermatologist in an elaborate Medicare fraud scheme to falsely diagnose patients with conditions requiring expensive treatment programs. Prosecutors say Dr. Ana Caos wrote hundreds of thousands of dollars in unnecessary prescriptions, which were used by associates to bill Medicare for drug treatments never administered.

Securities Fraud

A federal grand jury indicted Rodrigo Molina of Miami and Marcos Macchione of Aventura for their alleged involvement in an international securities fraud operation based in Brazil. Prosecutors say the pair assisted a criminal ring that scammed $50 million from foreigners by promoting worthless stocks and shares in non-existent companies.

Consumer Fraud

Arthur Vanmoor of Boca Raton was sentenced to more than 17 years in prison for peddling fake cures for cancer, migraines and other ailments. Prosecutors say Vanmoor and his associates devised an elaborate consumer fraud scheme to sell and promote bogus medical products through an online marketing network.

THE VALUE OF
FLORIDA FRAUD

Florida's top industries and where selected illegal activities would rank. Florida GDP (2006): $713.5 billion.

Industry	Value (billions)	Share of GDP
Services	$231.7	32.5%
Finance, insurance & real estate	170.6	23.9
Government	78.9	11.1
Retail trade	56.6	7.9
Construction	55.8	7.8
Wholesale trade	47.0	6.6
Illegal activity (1)	36.7	5.1
Occupational fraud (2)	36.7	5.1
Manufacturing	35.9	5.0
Information	28.8	4.0
Transportation & public utilities	29.9	4.2
Medicare fraud (3)	12.0	1.7
Trade-based money Iaundering (4)	8.2	1.1
Agriculture, forestry & fishing	6.3	0.9

Source: Enterprise Florida

Estimates:
(1) International Monetary Fund
(2) Association of Certified Fraud Examiners
(3) U.S. Department of Justice
(4) John Zdanowicz, Florida International University

INTERNET FRAUD

Top five states by share of internet perpetrators (2007).

State	% of U.S. Internet Fraud
California	15.8%
Florida	10.1
New York	9.9
Texas	7.0
Illinois	3.6

Source: 2007 Internet Crime Report, Internet Crime Complaint Center, prepared by FBI and National White Collar Crime Center.

INSURANCE FRAUD

Insurance fraud convictions by state (2006).

State	Insurance Fraud Convictions
California	1,717
Florida	606
New York	473
New Jersey	364

Source: Coalition Against Insurance Fraud

2

The Lure of White-Collar Crime

Dana L. Turner and Richard G. Stephenson

Security managers must find ways to prevent, investigate and prosecute white collar crime, an increasing phenomenon that is not likely to disappear in the near future. A conservative estimate places the loss to businesses due to white-collar crime at $40 billion. The increasing incidence of white-collar crime may be attributed to many factors, including lax laws, inadequate emphasis on loss prevention, reluctance to report questionable practices and lack of professional ethics.

White-collar crime is not going away. It is highly profitable, relatively risk-free, and almost socially acceptable. Since these crimes will not just disappear, security managers must find new ways to fight back through prevention, investigation, and prosecution.

White-collar crime probably costs U.S. businesses more than $40 billion each year. Statistics are unreliable, however, because many of these crimes are never reported. White-collar crime is also responsible for a significant loss in productivity that is not reflected in the statistics. Disruption is inevitable after a crime has been committed. Therefore, competitiveness is reduced even more than the numbers indicate.

White-collar crimes are those committed without the use or threat of force and without the risk of physical harm to the victim or the criminal. Also, a person who abuses his or her position for personal financial gain is considered a white-collar criminal. An example of this is an attorney who uses his or her influence to convince a person suffering from Alzheimer's disease to include the attorney in the will as a beneficiary.

The lure of white-collar crime (Fraud), by Dana L. Turner and Richard G. Stephenson (1993). Security Management, Feb. 1993 v37 n2 p57 (2). Copyright © 1993 ASIS International, 1625 Prince Street, Alexandria, VA 22314. Reprinted with permission from the February 1993 issue of Security Management magazine.

24

Motives of white-collar criminals include a drug, gambling, or upscale lifestyle habit; large medical expenses or past-due bills; revenge against an employer; and just plain greed.

White-collar crimes may be perpetrated by the following:

* Individuals against other individuals. Most of these crimes have been committed by people in a position of authority and control, such as family members, attorneys, real estate, and insurance, agents, conservators, and physicians.

* Insiders against their organization. Internal criminals include business partners, office managers, computer programmers, stockbrokers, and senior executive officers.

* External criminals. External criminals include forgers, counterfeiters, computer hackers, industrial spies, and office supply pirates.

Whether internal or external, white-collar criminals' tactics include trickery, deceit, or misrepresentation. Some familiar schemes are customer impersonations, medical and insurance frauds, real estate and banking swindles, and embezzlements. The crimes may involve forged or counterfeit checks, receipts, business records, or other legal documents, or the criminals may be aided by technologies, such as on-line computer terminals, fax machines, and color copiers.

The white-collar criminal is generally a calculating risk taker who weighs the potential risk against the potential profit. If a criminally motivated person believes that the opportunity to make a profit is greater than the potential risk associated with discovery, it is crime time.

The motivation to commit a crime has increased in recent years as reports have revealed the vast wealth accumulated by tax cheaters and crooked savings and loan officers. This motivation is bolstered by the belief that white-collar criminals usually do not get caught. If they do, the punishment is light, and the social stigma is insignificant.

White-collar crime can have a significant financial payoff, but what are the risks?

IDENTIFICATION

The criminal must be identified in order to be prosecuted. In a society where people often do not look at each other while walking on the sidewalk and where recording a driver's license number on a check is more important than identifying the writer, this is usually a minor issue for external criminals. It is a greater issue, however, for internal criminals.

To help identify a criminal, employees should remember to pay equal attention to all details of any internal or external transaction, including the other employees involved, the transacting employee's level of authority, the customer, the setting, the type of identification, and the payment method used.

APPREHENSION

If the criminal is identified, the local law enforcement agency is usually responsible for conducting the initial investigation. The majority of the nation's police and sheriff's departments are generalist departments; they do not have, nor can they afford, specially trained personnel to handle white-collar crime.

Security managers should plan their investigations as if they are to receive no assistance from local law enforcement. That means conducting a thorough investigation, complete with documentation and followup.

PROSECUTION

Once a subject is apprehended and the elements of the crime are established, prosecution can begin. The prosecuting agency is usually responsible for conducting these legal proceedings. The majority of the nation's prosecuting agencies, however, are generalist departments also.

Security managers should assist the prosecutor as much as possible by delivering the most complete investigative package possible and ensuring the company is represented in all court-related matters.

RECOVERY

If the subject is found guilty and convicted, the court can order restitution to the victim. However, prosecutors often do not seek convictions on all counts of a multiple-count case, and the court can only order restitution on counts that result in convictions. Even then, assets must be located, liens must be filed, and property must be seized. Often both internal and external criminals have no recoverable assets.

White-collar crime is big business, and the nation has allowed this business to grow. Significant segments of entire legitimate and criminal industries have been built around white-collar crime. It generates sizable illegitimate income for a number of external criminals. Consider the following examples:

* The robber who steals a wallet at gunpoint for immediate cash or steals property only to sell it for cash. The victim's checks, credit cards, identification, and household property, however, are not worthless to him or her. The robber or burglar simply re-sells those items to another criminal--a middleman--who then sells them to a third criminal who has the skill to use them to turn a profit.

* A prostitute may sell compromising client information to an extortionist; checks and credit cards to a re-seller; and sensitive business information to an industrial spy.

* The industrial spy who eavesdrops on employees' conversations at their favorite (and habitually frequented) restaurant may have no personal use for the sensitive information the employees discuss but that information may be worth a lot of money to a competitor.

White-collar crime also generates a sizable legitimate income for numerous legitimate businesses and government agencies. If white-collar crime disappeared overnight, the negative impact on the nation's economy would be significant. For example, consider the effect of the elimination of white-collar crime on the following industries:

Criminal justice system. How much of the local, state, and federal budget is dedicated to the investigation, prosecution, defense, and punishment of white-collar criminals? How many police officers, investigators, lawyers, judges, court clerks, probation officers, and jailers owe their livelihoods to white-collar criminals?

Media. How much of the media's time is dedicated to crime reporting, particularly addressing white-collar crime? How much of that reporting glorifies the exploits of white-collar criminals and the way they live?

Insurance and bonding companies. How much of these companies' profits result from the payment of premiums related to appearance bonds, fidelity bonds, and similar insurance coverage?

Internal security personnel and consultants. How many individuals are employed to provide internal security, training, and consulting services to businesses concerned about their exposure to white-collar crime?

The news is filled with reports of white-collar crimes. The savings and loan industry has suffered from fraud and insider abuse; the defense industry has been racked by overcharges and failed product designs; public and private universities have been plagued with overcharges and inappropriate charges for government-sponsored research; the House of Representatives' post office and bank have been misused; major retailers have suffered from huge embezzlement losses; national membership associations have been riddled with pyramid schemes and debt-saddling prior to bankruptcy filing; national nonprofit charitable organizations have had dues and donations converted to political action committees (PACs) and individual use; and securities brokerage firms have suffered through insider trading and other fraudulent practices.

Individuals who commit these crimes have the opportunity to earn a comfortable living. If apprehended and convicted, the criminal faces only a small risk of significant prison time, which may be served in a relatively comfortable minimum security prison. This treatment sends a clear message to anyone who has ever thought of committing a white-collar crime: While society recognizes that certain behavior is not honest, it is more acceptable than other types of crime. This is an extremely dangerous lesson, one that sets the stage for the actions that follow. Have these white-collar criminals become role models?

External white-collar criminals often work within a gang. The most powerful criminals are honored by the members with special privileges not afforded to the rest of the group. Internal white-collar criminals are not so different. They often work within an analogous gang structure, rise to power using comparable tactics, abuse similar privileges, and serve equally as role models.

Executives, managers, business owners, and security personnel often contribute--consciously or unconsciously--to the emergence of white-collar crime in their businesses. Their personal conduct often sets a poor example, and their policies provide the windows of opportunity. They fail to establish effective internal controls, they do not properly document procedures, and they inadequately train employees.

The following is a list of the most prevalent factors contributing to both the internal and external white-collar crime problem:

* Ineffective written policies and procedures governing all aspects of the business

* Inadequate emphasis on loss prevention and operational security

* Ineffective internal controls to identify errors, protect honest employees, and identify suspects

* Inadequate investment in employee training, both in routine operational and loss prevention-specific strategies and tactics

* Lack of a clearly written code of business and professional conduct that establishes a standard for all employees

* Ineffective screening of potential employees, vendors, and customers

* Inappropriate focus on technological methods to reduce losses while simultaneously decreasing the reliance on human skills

* Reluctance to report crimes affecting the business, resulting in an understatement of the problem's scope

* Insufficient emphasis on prosecution of perpetrators

* Inadequate sharing of loss prevention strategies, techniques, and history between similar businesses

A successful defense against white-collar crime begins with a single action by one concerned person. Someone must take a stand against the white-collar criminal and then be able to encourage others to take a stand. White-collar criminals will continue to thrive until industry leaders acknowledge the magnitude of the problem, deem this activity intolerable, and take an active role in prevention and education.

Dana L. Turner is a partner in Security Education Systems in Palo Cedro, California, and a member of ASIS. Richard G. Stephenson is a partner in the law firm of Troughton & Soter in San Francisco, California.

3

The Challenge of White Collar Sentencing

Ellen S. Podgor

Sentencing white collar offenders is difficult in that the economic crimes committed clearly injured individuals, but the offenders do not present a physical threat to society. This Article questions the necessity of giving draconian sentences, in some cases in excess of twenty-five years, to nonviolent first offenders who commit white collar crimes. The attempts by the U.S. Sentencing Commission to achieve a neutral sentencing methodology, one that is class-blind, fails to respect the real differences presented by these offenders. As the term "white-collar crime" has sociological roots, it is advocated here that sociology needs to be a component in the sentencing of white collar offenders.

I. INTRODUCTION

White collar offenders in the United States have faced sentences far beyond those imposed in prior years. For example, Bernard Ebbers, former CEO of WorldCom, was sentenced to twenty-five years; Jeffrey Skilling, former CEO of Enron, was sentenced to twenty-four years and four months; and Adelphia founder John Rigas received a sentence of fifteen years, with his son Timothy Rigas, the CFO of the company, receiving a twenty-year sentence.

These greatly increased sentences result in part from the employment of the United States sentencing guidelines structure, which includes in the computation of time the amount of fraud loss suffered. Although the sentencing guidelines have some flexibility resulting from the recent Supreme Court decision in United States v. Booker, the culture of mandated guidelines still permeates the structure and, as such, prominently advises the judiciary. Equally

The challenge of white collar sentencing, by Ellen S. Podgor. (2007). Journal of Criminal Law and Criminolgy, Spring 2007, v97 i3 p731 (29). Reprinted by permission. Footnotes have been removed.

influential in these sentences is the fact that because parole no longer exists in the federal system, the time given to these individuals will likely be in close proximity to the sentence that they will serve.

Although many are quick to denounce the conduct of these individuals and desire lengthy retributive sentences, their disgust with this criminality often overlooks a commonality among these white collar offenders. Each of these individuals has no history of prior criminal conduct. The corporate white collar offenders of today are typically individuals who have never been convicted of criminal conduct and are now facing incredibly long sentences as first offenders. The sentences imposed on these first offenders for economic crimes can exceed the sentences seen for violent street crimes, such as murder or rape.

In an effort to crack down on white collar criminality, the courts and legislature have produced draconian sentences that place prominence on the activity involved. In contrast to the approach taken with recidivist statutes such as "three strikes" laws, the focus in white collar sentencing is on the offense, with little recognition given to the clean slate of these offenders.

This Article, in Section II, traces the history of the term "white collar crime," noting its sociological roots. It contrasts this approach with the way the term "white collar crime" is used today. This section recognizes the deficiencies in a biased methodology that uses factors such as a person's wealth to determine whether the person should face criminal charges or punishment. It notes, however, that a rejection of bias in the sentencing process does not necessitate the elimination of all sociological considerations, especially those that might promote legitimate differences. Section III moves to a discussion of the white collar offender in the corporate world. It looks at the realities and risks faced by this offender in light of the federal sentencing system of today. Section IV extends this discussion, looking at factors that could enhance sentencing in white collar cases. Offered are sociological considerations that provide alternatives to the cold numerical system of "loss" as the key element used in determining the sentence of a convicted white collar offender. Although some of this discussion applies equally to other federal offenders, especially those sentenced in drug cases, the focus of this piece is exclusively on white collar crime.

White collar sentences need to be reevaluated. In an attempt to achieve a neutral sentencing methodology, one that is class-blind, a system has evolved in the United States that fails to recognize unique qualities of white collar offenders, fails to balance consideration of both the acts and the actors, and subjects these offenders to draconian sentences that in some cases exceed their life expectancy. In essence, the mathematical computations that form the essence of sentencing in the federal system fail to recognize the sociological roots of white collar crime.

II. WHITE COLLAR CRIME: DEVELOPING THE SOCIOLOGICAL ROOTS

White collar crime is a relatively new concept. Yet despite its recent vintage, it has not been consistently approached by all constituencies. Initially a sociological concept, "white collar crime" is recognized today as a legal term. Translating the sociological concept into a legal one presents deficiencies when placed in the context of the federal sentencing guidelines structure.

A. Sutherland's Approach

Crucial to any discussion regarding white collar crime is an understanding of its meaning. This term was initially a sociological term coined by sociologist Edwin Sutherland, whose theme was to recognize crime committed by individuals in positions of power. Although the examples in his initial book were limited to corporations, he argued generically that improper activities in this context should not be considered merely civil wrongs. This was criminal conduct, and he wanted it designated as such.

Sutherland looked at the offender in designating the conduct as criminal and used a class-based component in his definition. He factored the individual's "high social status" into his definition. Sutherland's sociological approach to white collar crime emphasized criminal acts by those in the "upper socioeconomic class," advocating that these individuals should not escape criminal prosecution.

What is perhaps the most interesting aspect of Sutherland's work is that a scholar needed to proclaim that crimes of the "upper socioeconomic class" were in fact crimes that should be prosecuted. It is apparent that prior to the coining of the term "white collar crime," wealth and power allowed some persons to escape criminal liability.

B. Department of Justice Approach

Since Sutherland's 1939 speech to the American Sociological Society and his later book on the topic of white collar crime, there have been many definitions used to explain this category of crime. In contrast to the offender-based approach favored by Sutherland, the more recent legal definitions of white collar crime focus on the offense. As such, tax evasion can be a white collar crime irrespective if it is the hotel owner who fails to report all of her income or the waiter who fails to report all of his tips. Arguably, an offense-based approach allows for a neutral methodology that is not influenced by a person's class and is not conditioned on political or corporate influence.

What is particularly problematic about the existing offense-based approach is that there is no list of white collar offenses. Thus, arguing that the act determines the designation but having no clear list of crimes included and excluded leaves one not knowing if a crime should or should not be considered when discussing the topic of white collar crime. This problem is perhaps exacerbated by the increasing number of offenses in the federal system, many of which exist outside of Title 18, the federal criminal code.

White collar crime definitions often recognize the economic nature of this type of crime. Key components tend to be "deception and absence of physical force." But when examining a criminal statute such as the Racketeer Influenced and Corrupt Organizations Act (RICO), determining whether the offense fits the white collar crime category may be dependent on the specific conduct involved. If the conduct is fraud and the predicate act is mail or wire fraud, it should be designated as a white collar crime. When, however, the RICO predicate relates to a state-based offense such as murder or robbery, it should clearly be outside the realm of being a white collar crime. As such, looking at the specific statute in the abstract may not determine whether the activity should be called a white collar crime. The circumstances of the conduct may be equally important in categorizing the activity.

One finds a noticeable discrepancy in the way the Department of Justice (DOJ) recognizes white collar crime. First, in DOJ literature, there is no explicit category called "white collar crime," yet there is continual usage of this term. Second, the Trac Reporting System of the DOJ includes antitrust and fraud as white collar crime but fails to include corruption as well as a host of other criminal activity that most people would consider as belonging to this category. The DOJ also does not include environmental offenses, bribery, federal corruption, procurement corruption, state and local corruption, immigration violations, money laundering, OSHA violations, or copyright violations as white collar crime. Each of these forms of criminal conduct is reported in separate categories exclusive of white collar crime. Thus, when the Trac Reporting System finds a "decline of about ten percent from FY 2003 to FY 2004" in white collar crime, the omission of many categories raises doubts about the accuracy of the reporting methodology.

Even subdivisions of the DOJ do not concur with the existing reporting system. For example, the United States Attorney's Office for the Northern District of California includes public corruption within its prosecutions of white collar crime. This same office also includes environmental offenses, as well as crimes concerning the Food and Drug Administration as white collar crime, and reports on their white collar prosecutions explicitly using this designation.

C. An Unbiased Sociological Approach

Historically, class was a component of the definition of white collar crime. The offender's position of power allowed the person committing the crime to be labeled a white collar offender. With the present focus on the offense, the accused's background, uniqueness, and circumstances often are omitted in categorizing the crime as either a white or non-white collar crime.

An offense-based approach, as opposed to an offender-based approach, provides the clearest attempt to achieve neutrality. It eliminates class, political influence, gender, and race from determining whether individuals fall within the ranks of being designated a white collar offender. In omitting these biases, however, it may also fail to account for real differences that might need recognition to fully understand this category of criminal conduct. In moving to a strict offense-based analysis and discarding a sociological approach that is premised on improper biases, the existing system omits consideration of legitimate offender differences. This same problem is reflected in the federal sentencing system.

III. OFFENDER SENTENCING REALITIES AND RISKS

The white collar offender in the corporate sphere is usually a person with power, although the level of power within the corporate world can be very different depending on the person's rank and the corporate structure. He or she can be a CEO who has delegated the power to underlings or a corporate executive who prefers to maintain a high level of control. The offender can also be a rogue employee who seeks to secure individual profit without consideration of the harm being caused to others. Perhaps the saddest cases are those employees who commit criminal acts in an attempt to please their bosses or show their value to the company. This latter group can include those who receive no direct or consequential benefit from the criminal activity. They have the power to commit the illegal conduct but receive little reward.

This next section starts by looking at the individual offender and his or her culpability. Considered is the role of the offender in the timeline of corporate corruption and whether the individual had a self-profit motive for engaging in the criminal conduct. Finally, the realities of sentencing are discussed, including the risk of proceeding to trial or accepting the sure finality of a plea agreement.

A. The Offender

The defendants in corporate fraud accounting cases are basically law-abiding citizens who have not had criminal problems in the past. For example, both Bernard Ebbers and Jeffrey Skilling were first offenders. If defendants who commit corporate frauds had been caught early in their schemes, the damages might not have been as significant as represented in so many of these cases. The crimes committed by those in the corporate world often present larger social harms because of the great number of victims and the enormous economic loss to these victims. Clearly, many individuals lost pension funds and life savings as a result of these wrongdoings. Likewise, it is evident that sharp punishment is in order to deter this criminal conduct.

Defendants charged with corporate frauds seldom require a court-appointed attorney as their wealth places them in an above-average socioeconomic level. Yet because they are at the top, they have farther to fall.

In addition to the powerful position that these individuals may hold, white collar offenders can often be subject to collateral consequences. If lawyers, they are likely to lose their ability to practice law. If stockbrokers, it is unlikely that they will be able to return to their profession. And if part of the medical field, the government may exclude them from federal programs. Unlike the plumber or gardener, a white collar offender is often unable to return to his or her livelihood after serving imprisonment. Licensing, debarment, and government exclusion from benefits may preclude these professionals from resuming the livelihoods held before their convictions. White collar offenders often receive a higher sentence for having a skill, and they can suffer additionally by the collateral consequences that accompany that skill.

Re-entry into society can also be problematic for the white collar offender. While some criminal defendants may think of criminal charges as "catching a case," and, as such, acceptable in society, the white collar offender's country club society is often gone when the person completes his or her sentence. Also, because of the power and prestige held by the corporate-related offender, the person is more likely to feel a greater shame in the community. Being a "front-pager" can subject the individual to more scrutiny and negative publicity, something that might not be felt by individuals of lesser status in society.

Clearly these factors are not persuasive to the general public, as wealth, education, and prestige are often cited as reasons for giving white collar offenders a harsher punishment. The lack of sympathy from the general public makes white collar offenders easy targets for increased punishment.

B. The Offender's Culpability

There are a wide range of different offenders, each demonstrating different levels of culpability. One finds the mid- to upper-level executive who is heavily involved in the criminal conduct but does not hold the position of CEO. Then there is the CEO who may not be the one who devises the scheme but tolerates or promotes it by his or her high level in the company. There is also the mid- to lower-level individual who participates in the conduct for personal gain or promotion within the company but is not the key player in devising the corporate scheme. Finally, some white collar offenders commit their acts because they want to impress their superiors by showing inflated company profits. This last type of individual may not actually be receiving a personal benefit beyond company recognition.

An example of such a corporate white collar scenario is found in the story of Jamie Olis, the former Senior Director of Tax Planning and International at Dynegy, who later served as its Vice President of Finance. Olis "was in his third year at [Dynegy]" when he went to work on Project Alpha. "Project Alpha was a plan to borrow $300 million and make it appear to the outside world (and in particular to Dynegy's auditor Arthur Andersen) as if the money was generated by Dynegy's business operations." The fraudulent accounting scheme came to a halt when the "SEC required Dynegy to restate the cash flow as derived from a 'financing' rather than 'operations.'" The effect was that "Dynegy was now seen to be borrowing rather than earning money from Project Alpha." The scheme, involving special purpose entities, "a parent level hedge," and tear-up agreements, which were meant to protect banks from losing money, was suddenly facing a decreasing stock price.

Olis, along with his boss Gene Foster and co-worker Helen Sharkey, were indicted for their conduct relating to this accounting fraud. Foster, a key witness against Olis at his trial, and the individual who approved his work, received a sentence of fifteen months in return for his plea and cooperation. Sharkey received a sentence of one month. Olis, who did not enter a plea and went to trial, initially received a sentence of 292 months. This over-twenty-four-year sentence was given for convictions of securities fraud, mail and wire fraud, and conspiracy.

Despite having no prior criminal record, thus being a level one offender under the sentencing guidelines, Olis received this high sentence because the court determined that he caused a loss of $105 million to one shareholder, the University of California Retirement

System. The high sentence was also in part a function of the court finding that "Olis employed 'sophisticated means' and a 'special skill' to carry out the fraud; and that there were more than fifty victims of the fraud." Although the conviction was affirmed, the case was remanded for re-sentencing. Circuit Judge Edith Jones rejected the "district court's approach to the loss calculation" because it failed to "take into account the impact of extrinsic factors on Dynegy's stock price decline."

Olis was eventually re-sentenced to seventy-two months, with the court concluding "that it [was] not possible to estimate with reasonable certainty the actual loss to shareholders attributable" to the fraudulent scheme. The court chose to base the sentence instead on an "intended loss to the United States Treasury of $79 million."

In some cases, the defendants will have realized significant personal profits from the criminal conduct. Other cases, like that of Olis, have individuals seeking to enhance a company with insignificant personal benefit. The personal benefit may be limited to bonuses, promotions, or raises resulting from high company performance.

When a CEO or high-level executive stumbles onto fraudulent activity, discovering the fraud places the CEO in the difficult position of protecting the company while not perpetuating the activity. The court in United States v. Adelson described the former Chief Operating Officer and President of Impath, Inc., a company involved in cancer diagnosis testing, as having been "sucked into the fraud not because he sought to inflate the company's earnings, but because, as President of the company, he feared the effects of exposing what he had belatedly learned was the substantial fraud perpetrated by others." Judge Rakoff, the district court judge authoring the opinion in this case, took the bold step of moving away from the mathematics of the sentencing guidelines to factor in all aspects of offender culpability. The government, however, has filed a notice of appeal in this case.

The convicted defendants in all these cases were clearly speeding down the corporate highway. The fact that others might speed is irrelevant. The fact that there is no intent to hurt someone is also unimportant. The overriding fact is that they engaged in illegalities and a wreck occurred. If the sentencing guidelines are strictly adhered to, the consequences of the wreck determine the sentence imposed.

C. Caught in the Post-Sarbanes-Oxley Net

Most criminal laws are written reactively--an event happens, and Congress provides legislation to appease the public. Whether it be the Patriot Act, Megan's Law, or the Sarbanes-Oxley Act, the legislation in these instances was an outgrowth of the public outcry for retribution for criminal conduct. In some cases, the media influence and public desire for legislation are less noted, as when Congress passes laws requested by the DOJ to provide more efficient prosecution. For example, although mail and wire fraud statutes exist, Congress passed a health fraud statute that specifically authorizes prosecutions relating to the health care industry. Although a specific event did not trigger this legislation, the high cost of medical services may have influenced a reexamination of this industry.

The passage of new laws places certain individuals in greater jeopardy for being held criminally culpable. Although the United States prohibits ex post facto prosecutions, ongoing activity can become subject to new legislation after its passage. There is no grandfathering in of future criminal conduct. Thus, criminal activity that occurs after the passage of the statute becomes fair game for prosecutors.

Even without new legislation, prosecutors can use generic statutes to reach conduct that may not have been the subject of prior criminal prosecutions. As stated by Chief Justice Burger, "[w]hen a 'new' fraud develops--as constantly happens--the mail fraud statute becomes a stopgap device to deal on a temporary basis with the new phenomenon, until particularized legislation can be developed and passed to deal directly with the evil."

Further, when the criminal activity has a historical basis in a corporation or is part of the "corporate ethos," those initially caught in the government net provide the general deterrence for later violators. With sufficient notice of the criminal activity provided by the very passage of the legislation, the initial group of individuals prosecuted for crimes cannot successfully argue that they were deprived of due process notice. On the other hand, those prosecuted after these first few offenders have the benefit of hearing about the prosecutions to realize the impropriety of these acts. This is particularly important in white collar regulatory offenses, which might not, by their very nature, be immediately seen as criminal activity. This is also true for new business crimes that might, in prior years, have been subject only to civil penalties.

The bottom line is that the prosecution cycle needs to start somewhere and the unfortunate individual who happens to go first is just unfortunate. There is no credit received for being the initial recipient of criminal prosecution. After all, these individuals have engaged in criminal activity.

Those caught in the initial net thrown into the sea of criminal conduct are likely to be offenders who understood their conduct might not be proper but did not realize it could produce criminal charges and draconian sentences. Although the statutes used, such as mail or wire fraud, may have been on the books for many years, the statutes' application to this form of criminality may be new.

It is important to note here that in many instances, if corporate controls had been properly in place, the individual criminality would not have been able to pass under the radar. If, in fact, the corporation had an effective corporate compliance program, the criminality would have been seen well before the government prosecution. The federal sentencing reality, however, is that the guidelines do not consider the existence, or lack thereof, of general deterrent punishment education received by the offender. Although individuals may be at different places along the spectrum of government enforcement against fraudulent activity, this is irrelevant for sentencing purposes.

Individuals are sentenced by looking at the offense, with add-ons for items such as being a skilled person, being an organizer or leader, or obstructing the government's investigation. The guidelines allow for an increased sentence when the points accumulated raise the offense level. Although the guidelines provide a downward adjustment for someone in a minimal role, lack of notice of the criminal conduct, or belief that the activity is merely acceptable business conduct instead of criminal conduct, does not diminish the sentence under the guidelines. Culpability is to a large extent an "all-or-nothing" methodology--either the person committed the criminal conduct or did not.

D. Motive as a Sentencing Factor

The individual's motive in committing the crime may also be overlooked in the federal sentencing process. Although motive has never been a mandate of intent and may not be a factor in determining guilt or innocence, motive can be a consideration in punishment theory. The federal sentencing guidelines, however, do not for the most part examine the accused's motive, and only creative post-Booker courts have chanced going down this avenue. As such, the accused that causes an astronomical loss to the public but gains no individual profit may be treated in a similar manner to the individual who might be purchasing costly shower curtains for his home from the profits of his or her corporate fraud. Circuit Judge Evans, found in United States v. Corry that motive to the victim is "mostly irrelevant" and therefore not something to consider in sentencing. He stated, "[i]f someone steals your wallet and gives the money in it to the Humane Society, rather than blowing it in Las Vegas, that's little comfort as you gaze at your empty pocket."

Some judges, however, do consider the offender's motive in the sentencing computation. For example, in United States v. Ranum, the court fully examined the individual defendant, as opposed to merely the offense and the resultant use of a strict numerical computation. Ranum, a senior bank loan officer in charge of "managing a commercial loan portfolio and evaluating loan applications," was convicted of "misapplication bank funds." He received a year-and-a-day sentence for this criminal conduct, a sentence imposed shortly after the Court's ruling in Booker.

The district court rejected the prosecution request for a guideline sentence of thirty-seven to forty-six months and also rejected a defense request for home confinement. The judge specifically noted that the "defendant's culpability was mitigated in that he did not act for personal gain or for improper personal gain of another." Noting the aggravated sentence provided by the loss amount under the guidelines, the court stated that "[o]ne of the primary limitations of the guidelines, particularly in white-collar cases, is their mechanical correlation between loss and offense level." The court noted that "[i]t is true that, ... from the victim's perspective the loss is the same no matter why it occurred." The court in Ranum then stated that "from the standpoint of personal culpability, there is a significant difference."

In Ranum, the court considered the history and character of the defendant. Additionally, factors normally omitted in federal sentencing discussions were mentioned in this case. Significantly, the sentencing decision was not a mathematical equation but rather presented consideration of culpability beyond noting that the individual was within Category One. The court recognized that the accused did not act with a personal motive.

E. Risking Trial

In addition to the loss factor being a crucial component in determining a sentence, the extent that a person will be punished is also contingent on whether the individual risks a trial. Those who go to trial and are not acquitted face incredibly high sentences. In contrast, those who work with the government and accept a plea with cooperation can reduce their sentences substantially. One need only look at the disparity in sentences between Jeffrey Skilling's sentence of twenty-four years and four months following a trial and Andrew Fastow's six-year sentence following a plea and cooperation with the government. As such, in making the decision to proceed to trial, individuals who believe themselves innocent face enormous sentencing risks should the jury think otherwise. Although courts are instructed to "avoid the unwarranted sentence disparities among defendants with similar records who have been found guilty of similar conduct," cooperation can serve as a "reasonable explanation" for a noticeable sentencing differential.

Miami banker Eduardo A. Masferrer is an example of an individual who took the risk of trial. Masferrer was convicted after a jury trial for his role in a twenty million dollar bank fraud that included concealing the criminal activity from regulators. He received a sentence of thirty years, while the bank president, Juan Carlos Bernace, who took the route of a plea, received a six-and-a-half-year sentence. Defense counsel questioned this disparity.

Taking the risk of going to trial may not be a determination solely within the province of the individual defendant. As prosecutors tend to work up the ladder in proceeding against criminal activities, those who are higher in the corporate hierarchy often stand a greater chance of receiving a higher sentence. Likewise, those with little or nothing to offer the government in their plea negotiation may not realize the full benefits that can accompany government cooperation. These factors have been the subject of concern long before the recent sentencing of white collar offenders.

Some cases have defendants arguing that higher-ups knew of the wrongdoing and approved the activity, while other cases have CEO defendants arguing that they did not know the criminality was occurring under their reign. This theme can be seen with defendants such as Bernard Ebbers, former CEO of WorldCom, and Kenneth Lay, former CEO of Enron, who were both convicted after a jury trial. Richard Scrushy, former CEO of HealthSouth, was initially acquitted by a jury.

Individuals taking the risk of going to trial are not usually schooled in the realities of the criminal process and the prison system, as they are first offenders. Deciding whether to take the risk may also be a function of money, as the cost of legal counsel can influence the ability to spend the sums necessary for a trial, thus forcing a plea negotiation to preserve assets for the offender's family.

Sentencing in the federal system does not account for the risk taken by the individual who goes to trial. In fact, it works against this person by having him or her receive a higher sentence than could have been obtained if the defendant had not demanded enforcement of the constitutional right to a jury trial.

An additional factor that compounds this risk is the recent flux of deferred prosecution agreements. These agreements provide the corporation with a benefit, often to the detriment of the individual. The government leverages the corporation against the individual, demanding total cooperation in its investigation. Corporations agreeing to deferred prosecution agreements can sometimes become mini-prosecutors in an effort to appease the government.

IV. MEASURING WRONGFULNESS

The United States Sentencing Commission sets the parameters for a sentence. Although post-Booker the judiciary has some sentencing discretion, the mathematical equation under the guidelines is, more often than not, the norm. In recent years, sentences have increased for many white collar crimes. The United States Sentencing Commission's Final Report on the Impact of United States v. Booker on Federal Sentencing attributes two factors to the increased rate of imprisonment in the fraud/theft category. First is the fact that "statutory and guideline penalties increased for many fraud offenses as a result of the Commission's Economic Crime Package of 2001, the 2002 Sarbanes-Oxley Act and other recent legislation."Second is the increased number of prosecutions. The reality of the sentencing guidelines' uniformity is that new legislation ratchets up sentences to an overall higher level. Also apparent is that imprisonment is the norm, with little respect given to alternatives that might better rehabilitate individual wrongdoers.

　　　This next section starts by looking at a pre-guidelines study of sentencing in white collar cases. It considers the deficiencies of the existing guideline system, a system premised strictly on a mathematical formula with little consideration of the individual and his or her culpability. Argued here is that a system that employs a mathematical calculation to determine an individual's sentence omits proper recognition of the offender, the offense, and the need to protect society from future dangerousness.

A. Pre-Guideline Sentencing of White-Collar Offenders

The Yale White Collar Crime Studies of the late 1970s conducted interviews that looked at the judge's rationale in sentencing the non-white collar offender from that of the white collar offender. Professors Kenneth Mann, Stanton Wheeler, and Austin Sarat noted that there was a pronounced difference in the way judges sentenced white collar crime cases, with the focus being on general deterrence as opposed to other methodologies. They noted that "[m]ost judges share a widespread belief that the suffering experienced by the white-collar person as a result of apprehension, public indictment and conviction, and the collateral disabilities incident to conviction--loss of job, professional licenses, and status in the community--completely satisfies the need to punish the individual." (133) The study raised issues of "equity in the sentencing process," specifically noting aspects such as the "use of economic sanctions when the defendant can clearly pay for them--sanctions that are unavailable to the defendant who is poor."

In an article authored by Stanton Wheeler, David Weisburd, and Nancy Bode, the odd revelation is presented that "one's socioeconomic status is positively related to the severity of the sanction." In a post-Watergate world, judges were increasing the penalties of those who progressed through the system and were charged with a white collar offense.

B. Purely Mathematics

Much has changed in the legal landscape since the Yale studies, most notably with the institution of the guidelines. These guidelines have moved sentencing in a direction that embraces "uniformity." Loss controls the determination of the sentence, and there is little recognition given to individual offender characteristics.

In many cases, the high-profile corporate CEO or the individual unwilling to accept a plea and cooperate with the government receives a high sentence. This is in large part because of the fraud guidelines that use "loss" as a key factor in sentencing. As noted by Professor Peter Henning in discussing the sentencing of Bernard Ebbers, former CEO of WorldCom, "the determination of loss can raise a sentence quickly from modest to substantial." Despite the uncertainty in determining a "loss" value, the different approaches that exist, and the need to find that the fraud caused the loss, the numerical amount can often equate with a sentence that exceeds the person's life expectancy.

The "add-ons" to the loss calculation are equally quantitative. For example, a sentence can increase by two levels for ten or more victims, four levels for fifty or more victims, and six levels for 250 or more victims. In some instances, the additional "add-ons" are specific to particular conduct or a particular statute.

In a post-Booker world, courts have received some discretion in deciding the unreasonableness of a sentence. The extent to which appellate tribunals will permit this discretion to flourish remains to be seen. With white collar offenders bearing the brunt of society's scorn, using a classless charging and sentencing process remains attractive to the public.

C. Deficiencies of a Strict Quantitative Approach

The one-size-fits-all methodology of sentencing white collar offenders seriously diminishes consideration of the individual offender, the nature of the offense, and the level of protection needed to satisfy the public's interest. It provides a mathematical computation for determining the sentence without regard to sociological differences.

1. Failure to Consider the Offender

The federal sentencing guidelines fail to adequately examine the individual offender in determining the sentence. Omitted from consideration are the collateral consequences faced by the offender and the differences he or she faces upon re-entry into society. The specific culpability of the individual also is not considered. Courts do not focus on whether the accused had the benefit of seeing prior individuals receive harsh penalties and thus was able to have the benefit of deterrence prior to their committing the act, or, alternatively, whether the accused was caught committing the crime du jour without realizing that the activity is not acceptable business conduct.

Culpability is basically non-existent as a sentencing concern, with the punishment resting on a numerical figure that correlates with the amount of loss occurring as a result of the crime. Courts seldom consider where the individual may be on the corporate ladder, the extent to which he or she is directly engaged in the criminal conduct, and any individual profit obtained as a result of engaging in the improper activity. In essence, sentencing fails to account for a difference between the CEO heavily entrenched in the criminal behavior and the CEO with little knowledge of criminal wrongdoing. Also omitted from the review process is the motivation of the accused and the actual benefit received by this individual.

2. Failure to Consider the Uniqueness of White Collar Crimes

The failure to focus on the offender is exacerbated by the fact that the crimes used in white collar cases have little or no flexibility. Unlike many state offenses, there are no degrees or lesser included offenses to these crimes. For example, a homicide can be many different crimes dependent upon factors such as heat of passion, deliberation, premeditation, cooling off period, or extreme emotional disturbance. Irrespective of the jurisdiction or the grading methodology used, the offense level is adjusted by the culpability of the accused. An unlawful killing can range from being considered murder in the first degree, voluntary manslaughter, or reckless homicide, to perhaps a vehicular homicide, depending on the specific laws of the jurisdiction.

One does not find these lesser included offenses with white collar crimes as there are no degrees or levels of punishment. The classic white collar crimes--bank fraud, mail fraud, and wire fraud--are not predicated on lower level crimes with a lesser degree of culpability or extenuating circumstances. The individual is either guilty or not guilty of the designated offense.

3. Future Dangerousness

Perhaps the most noticeable characteristic omitted by the quantitative approach to sentencing is future dangerousness. White collar offenders, especially those coming from the corporate arena, are usually first offenders. Additionally, there is little likelihood of recidivism. The individual seldom can resume a position of power that would allow for continued criminality of this nature.

The court also has the ability to limit any future dangerousness by precluding the individual from serving in a future corporate position. For example, in his sentencing of Richard P. Adelson, former Chief Operating Office and President of Impath, the Honorable Jed Rakoff stated that "[w]ith [Adelson's] reputation ruined by his conviction, it was extremely unlikely that he would ever involve himself in future misconduct. Just to be sure, however, the Court, as part of the sentence here imposed, barred Adelson from ever again serving as an officer or director of a public company."

If sentencing has as a goal the protection of society, factoring in the future dangerousness of the individual is an important component of the system. With the elimination of the individual's corporate role, the stripping of the convicted felon's money, and the accompanying collateral consequences, such as a loss of license or ability to conduct business with the government, future dangerousness is nearly eliminated.

V. CONCLUSION

All of criminal law revolves around punishment theory. We create laws in order to punish conduct that society finds abhorrent. We then enforce these laws and punish offenders in order to secure adherence to the laws. The classic theories consider utilitarian models that encompass goals of deterrence, both general and specific, rehabilitation, isolation, and education. On the other hand, there is retributive theory that punishes for the sake of "paying the debt to society." Punishment theory is also multidimensional, with considerations of communicative retribution looking at not only the specific wrongs to victims but also the repercussions to society and groups within society that might suffer as a result of the wrongful act.

Sentencing of offenders is the last stage of punishment theory. It is the one portion of the criminal process when the court can examine individual culpability in relation to the offense committed. De-emphasizing this consideration because of concerns that class may play a factor in the sentence works to eliminate considerations unique to many corporate white collar offenders. Sentencing needs to remain fluid to account for all considerations and yet also be transparent for review. Most importantly, we need to infuse into the sentencing process some of the sociological teachings that started the discussion of white collar crime. It is important to strive for a sentencing system that is classless, but in doing so it is also important to respect real differences.

Ellen S. Podgor, Associate Dean of Faculty Development and Distance Education, Stetson University College of Law. The author thanks the participants in the Culverhouse Chair Lecture, the Oxford Roundtable, and the Fifteenth Annual National Seminar on the Federal Sentencing Guidelines. She also specifically thanks Professors Robert Batey, Douglas Berman, Peter Henning, and Michael Seigel for their comments throughout the drafting of this paper and also research assistant Todd Howard. Finally she thanks Dean Darby Dickerson and Stetson University College of Law for their support throughout the writing of this Article.

Part 3

Specialty Courts

1

How Drug Courts Reduce Substance Abuse Recidivism

Utah, The Public's Health and the Law in the 21st Century: Third Annual Partnership Conference on Public Health Law - Panel Discussion

Kirk Torgensen

Public health has been focused on bioterrorism and quarantine; however, the position put forward today is that substance abuse addiction is the greatest threat to the public's health. At the core of so many of society's problems is substance abuse. The common denominator in so many violent crimes and property crimes is addiction to some substance.

It is highly unlikely that a bioterrorist attack will take place in Utah. But today, and every other day of the year, methamphetamines are being cooked in various homes and apartments throughout Utah. Individuals are struggling with addictions to alcohol, cocaine, and a variety of other substances. Young children are being neglected and abused in homes where drugs are being concocted and consumed. And it is happening in every other state.

The criminal justice system tells the story. One indicator is recidivism. Approximately 80-85 percent of the inmates in the state of Utah have major substance abuse problems, and 80 percent of those get little or no treatment whatsoever for these problems. Seven out of ten prison parolees recidivate within two years. Our prison populations are growing immensely because people rarely leave the prison system permanently. At a cost of $30,000 per inmate per year,

How drug courts reduce substance abuse recidivism (Utah). The public's health and the law in the 21st century Third annual partnership conference on public health, by Kirk Torgensen. Journal of Law, Medicine, and Ethics, Winter 2004, v32, issue 4, p S69 (4). Reprinted by permission of Wiley.

Department of Corrections' budgets are consuming state budgets. And while this cost grows, the share of tax dollars left for education, health care, and other essential programs is diminishing. We need to wake up.

Last year in Utah one-half of all homicides committed were the result of domestic violence, and one-half of those were directly related to substance abuse--alcohol or some other drug. The driving factor behind the need to terminate parental rights is problems with substance abuse and addiction. Studies show that the vast majority of identity theft crimes are committed by those who are feeding their substance abuse addictions. If all we do is put these people in jail, make them serve their time, and release them back to their problems while still struggling with addiction, we, as a society, will lose this fight.

It is estimated that 3-5 percent of the drugs being shipped into the United States are intercepted by law enforcement officials; the other 95-97 percent succeed in entering the United States. We have come to realize that we cannot stop the international drug cartels. We cannot line the borders with enough police and National Guard to inspect everything entering the country. So how do we curtail this problem? We must first realize what the problem is. It is demand. There is an enormous demand for drugs in our country. As we recognize the problem, then we realize that we need a different approach to fighting the war on drugs. We need to make reducing the demand a priority. Otherwise we will continue to build more prisons at the expense of education, health care, and various other vital programs.

Utah recognizes this problem and is attempting to deal with it. State Senator Chris Buttars, the next presenter, sponsored the Drug Offender Reform Act. This legislation procures treatment dollars from the state budget. This money is used to identify those with substance abuse problems early on and to divert them into programs that make sense--programs that won't cost the state $30,000 per person. Judges in Utah have complained that they would prefer to put people with substance addictions on probation so that they can receive treatment, but that there are either no treatment programs available or there is no space in those that are. Instead, the judges are forced to send these individuals to prison. While it is politically popular to be "tough on crime," Senator Buttars is convincing Utah that it needs to be "smart on crime."

Years ago, Salt Lake City established drug courts specifically for this purpose. Drug courts bring the judicial and criminal justice groups together with the substance abuse treatment professionals. Through intensive supervision, accountability, and substance abuse treatment, the drug courts focus on assisting offenders in overcoming the addiction and abuse problems that are the underlying cause of the criminal activity in this particular population.

Based on relatively long-term experience, the drug courts have seen a recidivism rate of only 17 percent, which stands in stark contrast to the typical recidivism rate of prison populations which is 60-70 percent. These statistics are typical of what can be found in any state that has implemented a similar program. The savings associated with cutting the criminal recidivism rate with drug courts are astounding. Viewing substance abuse as the number one public health threat and setting up programs to deal with it, results in better families, better schools, and a better society.

Chris Buttars

In Utah, Criminal Justice, the Courts, and the Department of Corrections combined maintain the second largest budget in the state, approaching one billion dollars. For a small state like Utah, that is an enormous amount of money. Efforts are underway to enact the Drug Offenders Reform Act in the state. Utah, like many other states, has seen the beneficial effects of drug courts. The Drug Offenders Reform Act, or DORA, will build off of the drug courts' successful foundation and expand that system of reform to many other individuals with substance abuse problems in the state. Over a three-year period, DORA will phase in an intensive pre-screening assessment of all accused felons in the state. In order to qualify for the treatment program, individuals with substance abuse problems must, among other requirements, be non-violent, be a first- or second-time offender, and have some form of community support, whether it is family or a similar group.

Individuals recommended for the program based on their pre-screening assessment will be given the option of participating. Typically, a judge will agree to set aside an individual's plea and corresponding sentence if that individual agrees to fully participate in the program. The benefits to the offender are: staying home instead of prison, keeping a job (contributing tax dollars instead of merely consuming them), and receiving quality treatment for substance abuse addiction. The judge maintains leverage over the offender by retaining the option of reinstating the maximum sentence possible if the offender fails to fully cooperate in the treatment program.

The potential benefits to Utah are: savings of approximately $40 million dollars annually from DORA within three to four years of the program taking effect. Currently, the state prison system costs approximately $35,000 per inmate per year. It is estimated that 75-80 percent of the inmates have underlying substance abuse problems. Approximately 30-40 percent of those inmates with substance abuse

52

problems would qualify for the treatment program, which will cost approximately $3,500 per participant per year. This results in an annual savings to the taxpayers of $20 million dollars per 1,000 participants.

The comprehensive treatment programs encompassed in DORA are not politically popular in the beginning. Politically, leaders are expected to be "tough on crime," and out-of-prison substance abuse rehabilitation does not fit this image. But because of the success that Utahans have witnessed with drug courts in their state, many are anxious to expand this program to include additional non-violent criminals. When somebody gets busted for burglarizing a house or breaking into a car, sending them to jail is treating only the symptoms. Most of these offenders have broken the law in order to fund an expensive addiction. We can treat them and fix them, or we can send them to prison where they can learn how to become hardened criminals.

The change from imprisonment to treatment requires an enormous paradigm shift. For a long time, society's response to crime has been to lock up the offender. Some offenders need to be locked up for a long time; some are not locked up long enough. Some criminals are being released after only five years of a one-to-fifteen-year sentence simply to make room for newer criminals. Utah cannot afford to build more prisons. DORA will free up the space and resources to lock up the violent offenders and the sex offenders for the entire time they should serve.

The Drug Offenders Reform Act (DORA) enjoyed overwhelming support when it was first introduced in the state legislature last year. Remarkably, it received unanimous support in both the House and Senate Committees. It was voted through on the House floor, but then was tabled in the Senate because of bad timing-- the state was running a deficit. This year, however, Utah is projecting a $100 million surplus. The $6.5 million required to institute DORA's treatment programs will present little difficulty, particularly since it will result in tens of millions of dollars in savings over time. This year, DORA already has broad support in both houses of the state legislature. Groups fighting drugs and domestic violence have testified on DORA's behalf, and the vast majority of Utah's law enforcement agencies support the bill.

Utah will likely become the first state to pass this comprehensive treatment legislation. Although other states have experimented with drug courts and different types of rehabilitative treatment, none have a DORA-type program in place. In Texas, drug prisons have been successful. Drug prisons are designed for offenders with substance abuse problems who should not be placed with hardened criminals, but who should not be placed back in the community yet, either. The special prisons offer a therapeutic commune to those struggling to overcome addictions while serving time for their crimes.

In Utah, DORA will produce other savings in addition to the 90 percent reduction in expenditures for each participant. There are social services savings as well; for example, allowing an addicted mother to stay home with her child instead of making the child a ward of the state. The reduction in human suffering cannot be reduced to a dollar amount: it is priceless. It is time to become smart on crime.

Seth W. Norman

During the day, I hear a full criminal docket in Davidson County, Tennessee; at night, I serve as Nashville's Drug Court judge. During the day, I am tough on crime and have a reputation as being tough on those who come before me for sentencing. During the evening drug court call, my goal is to rehabilitate drug addicts and keep them out of prison cells. There is no inconsistency here: those who deserve tough sentences should get them, but ordering an addict to serve time accomplishes nothing.

It was seven years ago that I noticed a revolving door in Davidson County. I repeatedly sentenced individuals for drug infractions only to see them right back in the courtroom for similar violations as soon as their sentence was served. Although many people insisted that it was impossible to break a person's addiction to crack-cocaine, I felt that offering long-term treatment to addicts, instead of the traditional prison time, would prove effective. Hoping to confront Nashville's drug and crime problem from a different angle, my staff and I worked hard to set up a drug court. The Metro (Nashville) City Council passed a resolution devoting a former mental health hospital for use as a drug treatment facility as long as the drug court is in operation.

Not long after the former mental hospital was renovated for use as a drug treatment center, the mayor decided that a major international computer manufacturer wanted the premises and that the drug treatment center would have to close down. Citing the city council's resolution that permitted indefinite use of the former mental health hospital as a drug treatment facility, no one left. Consequently, Nashville found $3 million of urban renewal money to build a new residential treatment facility for the drug court, and the computer company was able to get the property it wanted.

After weathering its start-up years, Davidson County's Drug Court program is making its presence felt and gaining positive attention. While there are currently over 1,000 drug courts in the United States, Davidson County's is the only one that operates its

54

own residential treatment facility. The current facility has 100 beds--sixty for males and forty for females--and it is almost always at capacity. In addition, there are about twenty to thirty first-time offenders enrolled in an outpatient program. Because this system of treatment has proven to be so economical, discussions are underway with political leaders to establish additional drug courts and residential treatment facilities across the state. Other states have expressed interest in duplicating Nashville's success.

This is how the drug court program works: it is an option available to all non-violent offenders, most of whom have a long history of drug-related arrests. It is completely voluntary. The only requirements are that the offender must plead guilty to the charge, must have the prosecutor's consent, and must be willing to participate once admitted to the program. Although the underlying offense need not be drug-related, the offender must be addicted to drugs. The inpatient program usually lasts about fifteen months. The treatment facility has no guards, no locked doors, and no gates. Participants are told that they are free to escape if they want to; however, the maximum prison sentence will be reinstated and they may be prosecuted for escape, which adds an additional two years to their sentence. Few attempt to escape. For those few who do, they are easily apprehended. They are generally found buying drugs near the same corner where they were first arrested.

Drug treatment is a cost-effective option for the state. Because it is an unsecured facility, it costs less to maintain than a prison. Patients can be housed, fed, and treated for less than a prison can house and feed an inmate. While a typical prison inmate costs the state $52 per day, a patient at the treatment facility costs only $40 per day. That daily per capita savings adds up to approximately one-half million dollars each year. Last year, when the drug court's funding was cut and its budget was short by $600,000, it was brought to the state legislature's attention that without these funds, 100 drug court offenders would have to go to prison, increasing the state's corrections budget by $2.5 million. The legislature appropriated the funds, and the drug court/drug treatment program continues.

In addition to the federal funding of Davidson County's Drug Court, it receives operating expenses from other sources in the state. A portion of the district attorney's savings from not prosecuting the cases (because offenders who participate must plead guilty) is directed to the drug court. In addition, a Tennessee statute requires that each DUI ticket include a $100 "tax" which is to be used for drug treatment, and that money goes to fund the drug court.

Funding also comes from the participants themselves. The program requires that inpatients have a full-time, forty-hour-per-week job during the last three months of treatment. One-third of their income goes to the program for room and board; another third pays for court-related costs. The last third is for the patient's savings account and is payable upon graduation from the program.

There are also future savings--both monetary and social--to be considered. Treating these individuals now results in them becoming income-producing, tax-paying citizens; not treating this population results in physical, emotional, and psychological decline and eventual hospitalization. We can choose to pay now or to pay later.

The social benefits are significant as well. The General Accounting Office (now, the General Accountability Office) recently conducted a study that indicated a 70 percent recidivism rate within three years for untreated individuals in the penal system, nationwide. Every single patient who has participated in Davidson County's Drug Court program since 1997 is tracked every six months. This tracking system reports a 16-17 percent recidivism rate. In the program's seven-year existence, 300 individuals have graduated. Of the three hundred, less than fifty have been re-incarcerated, and only three have been re-incarcerated as a result of a violent crime. These are significant results. The legislature is noticing the benefits of this program. It is seeing drug court and residential treatment as an effective way to deal with drug offenders.

2

What Works and What Does Not: Drug Courts

Panel Discussion

Panelists:
Michael Rempel, Center for Court Innovation
Adele V. Harrell, The Urban Institute
Jeff Fagan, Columbia University School of Law
Barbara Babb, University of Baltimore School of Law

I want to talk about treatment modality and participant progress in recovery. Most of my examples are going to be regarding drug courts, with just one other kind of court, the domestic violence court. Of cases handled in the Bronx Misdemeanor Domestic Violent Court, seventy-five percent are mandated to a batterer intervention program.

There are a number of other types of programs--substance abuse treatment, alcohol treatment, combined programs--that are available. For instance, one type of combined program, batterer intervention and alcohol treatment, is a function of the existence of the domestic violence court in the Bronx. Recently that program was determined to be poorly run, so that's no longer used anymore. So variables that may not directly relate to treatment, but relate more to the relationships between the court and available treatment providers may affect the modality used.

There are actually four New York City drug courts. This just gives the distribution of first treatment modality for those four courts. Immediately you see that Brooklyn and Manhattan are fairly similar. Both start out by sending about half of their participants to a long-term residential program.

Queens sends far fewer to a residential program, and when you look at other data about Queens, you see that they have a

What works and what does not: Drug Courts. (2002) Fordham Urban Law Journal, June 2002, v 29, i5, p1929 (29). Reprinted by permission.

58

primarily young population, a population whose primary drug tends to be marijuana. So the clinical need is less, so they send fewer people to a residential program.

But then you get to the Bronx. Only four percent go to residential programs, eighty-five percent go to intensive outpatient. Well, that is not a function of clinical need. That is a function of the particular relationship between the court and treatment providers in the Bronx. In the Bronx, instead of referring out to a large number of treatment providers, they have a core of about ten to fifteen providers, all of which run intensive outpatient programs, some of which run other modalities.

But the dominant modality of treatment providers in the Bronx is intensive outpatient. Bronx courts tend to work very closely with these providers, so that the structural relationship between the court and those providers leads to an especially high degree of outpatient use.

I will just preview the results. If you were to look at retention rates across these courts, you could not necessarily conclude that one court is doing better or worse than the other based on modality they are using. But you would conclude that there are different types of relationships going on that are affecting the kinds of modalities being used.

Just to give a little bit of a overview of the other theme of the day that I want to talk to you about, I want to switch to the page that is titled "Graduate Compliance in the Brooklyn Treatment Court."

This is the other kind of necessity under treatment, that you have your modality, relationships between court and providers, and then in turn you have the participant response to that and their progress, not their outcomes but their progress, during the treatment and recovery process.

In this chart you see just the basic distribution of results for successful participants at the Brooklyn Treatment Court, and despite being; successful--everyone represented in this chart is a graduate-- only twenty-eight percent had zero positive drug tests during their participation; only thirty-eight percent had no unexcused treatment absences; and only fifteen percent avoided going out on a warrant.

Immediately you see that the recovery process tends to involve extensive relapses. And for any type of problem-solving court, that in turn raises the question of second chances: How many second chances are appropriate for the population you're working with? Are there types of third or fourth chances that are appropriate?

For instance, in this context in the Brooklyn Treatment Court, if there were no second chances, there would not be a particularly good graduation rate.

This sort of details the process a little bit more. This shows again just for graduates at the Brooklyn Treatment Court what their non-compliance rates are across five periods of their treatment: the first thirty days of treatment; between thirty and ninety days of treatment; after ninety days of treatment but prior to completing phase one of that program, which requires 120 days--and also, to complete phase one, that 120 days must be consecutive, drug-free, and sanctionless time--and then phase two and phase three.

Immediately you see, after just the first thirty days of treatment and a positive drug test, for an example, a tremendous improvement. After averaging a positive drug test on thirty-eight percent of tests in those first thirty days, immediately after participants are past that point, you get tremendous improvement in level of compliance.

There is one final point I want to make about treatment and recovery process. That was just for graduates. We did an analysis where we looked at graduates and dropouts, and the question is, what is a warning sign that someone is about to drop out?

We found that positive drug tests were completely not significant as a warning sign that someone was going to drop out. Continued use was not important. What was important was attendance, commitment to the recovery process, that the participants who did not go out on warrants, who did not miss treatment appointments, tended ultimately to succeed, even if they had multiple positive drug tests, whereas the participants that maybe improved in their drug use but didn't have the commitment to the recovery process tended ultimately to drop out. The participants with absences tended to drop out. But positive drug tests were not at all an indicator that someone was headed ultimately to fail the program.

That's a very brief snapshot of two process issues that, by and large, have not been analyzed extensively but that give you a flavor for where I think the next five years of research is going to be in problem-solving courts, less focus on do they work--they are here, we all know that--and more on how the treatment and recovery process goes, what modalities are used, and what is the course of recovery.

Adele V. Harrell The Urban Institute

I think the defining feature of problem-solving courts is the difference in the way they use legal coercion. Traditionally, courts have concentrated on using their authority to appropriately punish behaviors in the hopes that somehow that would deter future non-compliance. Problem-solving courts are really turning their attention directly on the subject of the offender's behavior, with less

60

concentration on the appropriate penalty for the immediate instant offense.

I think that change means that problem-solving courts have had to rethink our normal approach to research.

Deterrence theory is what most criminologists immediately turn to when they think about using legal pressure, and this sort of posits that people choose to comply or violate laws based on their perceptions of the costs and benefits associated with the behavior. There are three main components: the severity of the penalty they face, the certainty with which they will face it, and how quickly they will face it.

There are two types of deterrents, specific and general. Specific means that if you give the penalty to the person, they won't do it again. General means that the imposition of penalties will discourage others. Drug courts actually use this when they have people come to review hearings and watch other people being penalized. That's their effort at general deterrence.

What does the research say about it? It says certainty is the key; severity of punishment is important but not always significant, and it may depend on the certainty of punishment and on the salience of the penalty to the individual; and severity has rarely been found to have an effect on offender behavior.

I think what problem-solving courts need to do is switch and begin to think about what psychologists or behavior management theory has to say about the use of sanctions.

Important insights from that literature are that there are actually four kinds of sanctions. There are two kinds of positive sanctions and two kinds of negative sanctions.

There are rewards, which in drug courts are in the form of tokens and recognition, judicial praise. There is positive reinforcement. This means dropping something onerous that is going to happen to the person as a reward good behavior, such as requiring less appearances in court or fewer drug tests.

There are also punishments, which are in the form of graduated sanctions, which are immediate responses or penalties to negative behavior. And there is negative reinforcement, and that is the imposition of the penalty for failing to show the good behavior; that is, imposing the alternative sentence.

I think it is important to begin to think clearly about the different types of sanctions, and document what we are doing in these problem-solving courts that works.

The other insights from that literature are that the salience of the sanction varies by individuals. For example, one of the things you see in domestic violence research is that arrest is a deterrent for some people, those who are employed, and not for others.

The other insight from that literature is that contingency management is very important.

The principles of punishment are:

* A punishment must be severe enough to motivate efforts to avoid it.

* Punishment should be consistent, and should consistently follow unwanted behaviors.

* Punishments and negative reinforcement should be contingent upon offenders' behavior in a predictable and controllable way.

There are several implications for the way courts work. One is that this business of sending warning letters, for example, which is a first response to some drug court failures, may actually habituate offenders to the unwanted behavior because that's not very severe. So they get a free pass when they get a warning letter.

There is also an argument for making sanctions graduate in severity, because if the first one is not severe, maybe the second one is severe enough to motivate compliance.

Consistency is very important. Lab studies show that to the extent you deviate or give people free passes, it will actually discourage the learning or the emergence of the desired behavior.

With respect to punishments and negative reinforcements being contingent on offenders' behavior, not only do they need to be contingent but they need to be, from the offender's point of view, predictable and controllable.

That argues for the use of contingency contracts which spell out very clearly for your participant what the rules are, what they have to do to in behavioral terms very specifically. Such as they have to come to court, they have to go to the treatment program, not simply go away and be drug-abstinent or go away and go to treatment, but very specifically what they have to do.

Turning to the research on the effects of legal pressure, we see that there have been a number of studies that show that people who enter treatment under a legal mandate are more likely to stay in treatment, and stay in treatment longer. Review of long-term therapeutic communities, for example, showed this consistently. New York's DTAP program is an example. Mike Rempel's new analysis of Brooklyn Treatment Court data showed that people facing the most severe alternative sentence were more likely to enter treatment and complete the first phase of treatment, so that it was important in the treatment-engagement process.

62

Most of these studies are talking about negative reinforcement; that is, the consequence, the alternative sentence, that participants will encounter should they fail.

There is only one study that I know of that looked at graduated sanctions, which was our study of the D.C. Drug Court, which used penalties for specific behaviors. It was the only study that isolated the graduated sanctions or the punishment aspect of sanctioning.

It compared offenders who were randomly assigned to two dockets. In one docket, they got bi-weekly drug tests, lots of judicial monitoring, and encouragement to remain drug-abstinent. On the other docket, they got those same things and they were offered to join a graduated-sanctions program. Two thirds of participants chose to join the graduated-sanctions program, and this program spelled out in advance a set of rules. The rules specified that one positive drug test will result in the participant pending three days in the jury box; the second positive drug test results in three days in jail; the third positive drug test results in seven days in detox; and the fourth positive drug test results in seven days in jail.

These sanctions were applied with a great degree of consistency, so ninety-seven percent of the time, the offense was followed by the sanction, and most of the sanctions were delivered within a week.

What we saw was that the participants in the graduated sanctions program were three times as likely to test drug-free in the month before sentencing as those who were just getting judicial encouragement and drug testing.

I think that one of the lessons from that, though, was that when we did focus groups with the defendants, what they told us was that motivating them was the understanding up front of the behavioral rules of what they needed to do. The participants thought, therefore, it was an opportunity for them to show the judge what they could and could not do. They also accepted more readily the penalties when they were imposed.

However, the analysis also showed a significant interaction between graduated sanctions and those who voluntarily went to NA and AA meetings, which on both of the two dockets they were encouraged to do. But the sanctions had a very positive interaction with that, so that combining the voluntary treatment with the sanctions produced the best result.

Overall, I think this literature has several things to say about problem-solving courts. One is that they need to use the full range of sanctions--rewards, positive reinforcement, punishment, and negative reinforcement--and they need to be consciously thinking about how they're using each sanction.

The psychology literature indicates, of course, that the positive reinforcements are much more powerful motivators of behavior than negative reinforcements.

Courts need to consider sanction salience. It needs to be sufficient to motivate compliance. I think courts have to worry about not using muscle and therefore making sort of a joke of the program. They need to be sure that defendants understand that the sanctions are contingent on their behavior. Signed agreements are good.

Rules need to be enforced consistently, and rewards need to be given when appropriate. There is a tension in problem-solving courts between having a very rigid sanctions schedule, like that used in Washington, and tailoring those sanctions to the individual to encourage compliance. I think that we don't know yet what the right mix is of how best to maintain an appearance of fair rules and consistent rules but also be able to work with an individual who is struggling with addiction, and I think we really don't know where to draw that line.

We need to demonstrate consistency in sanction review hearings that are attended by all participants.

The other lesson from psychology, which I kind of glossed over because I was rushing, was that extralegal sources of reinforcement for legal pressure are very important, very important. For example, in the Puerto Rico drug court, they require a family member to stand at the review hearings with the defendant and talk about the family's encouragement of recovery and disappointment when recovery is not forthcoming.

Jeff Fagan Columbia University School of Law

For the past eighteen months, we have been studying the Community Justice Center in Red Hook, which is, for you non-New Yorkers, a neighborhood in Brooklyn, sort of southwest Brooklyn, which is physically and socially isolated, a very poor place, a long and rich history of both ups and downs, and a place that has pretty well been cut off from most social services and has had a history of government programs sort of coming in and going on.

That is an important backdrop, because it will explain a little bit about why this may or may not work. We don't know if it is working, and how we define "working" is an interesting question. But we're going to offer one theoretical perspective which will explain in part how we approached the question of "working".

It's more than just a problem-solving court; it's a community justice center. Community justice centers are very distinct from the kinds of drug treatment courts and batterer treatment courts and the like that we've heard about.

They are different in three important ways: They are forms of collective action by neighborhoods and citizens within neighborhoods, a set of reciprocal actions--what citizens do affects the courts, what courts do affects the citizens, what the citizens do affects the service providers, et cetera, et cetera.

One of the things that the community justice center attempts to do is to build a system of mutual accountability, which we think will ultimately leverage into a form of social control to reduce crime problems in the neighborhood.

Second, the court is in fact not just a court; it is a community program. It links service providers to the court; it links service providers to the families in way that are responsive to their perceived needs. It is physically and administratively closer to the social and behavioral problems that it seeks to address.

This is different than a problem-solving court. The physical stuff is not unimportant, it is extremely important, but equally important is that the court is now a service provider, a government agency in the community providing services. Some of those services are legal, some of those services are extralegal. How that works out will be an interesting question.

Third, the physical presence of the court in the community signals--and I use that in the Posnerian sense, for you law professors out there--that there are fact relationships of citizens to courts and to communities that differ in meaning and tone and content from the typical relationship that you see downtown or even in the problem-solving court, which is located in the Central Court Building.

We are focused on Red Hook, and Red Hook is a poor place with a long history. One of the recurring crises in Red Hook, and many neighborhoods like Red Hook, is a crisis of the legitimacy of the law, whether legal institutions generally are legitimate, and we define legitimacy in a way that people basically--the high political theorists would talk about the consent of people to be governed by these agencies that attempt to govern them, and we won't go into high theory today.

But we do think that problems in distributive justice--in other words, fairness and procedural justice--meaning the way people are treated, in addition to the failure or limitations of government programs generally to provide public safety in places like Red Hook has created a breach between citizens and government. That breach is reflected in citizen reactions to government and to programs like justice centers and other government agencies in the community.

Simply put, historically the police and the courts have not been allies of the communities in their fights for public safety, or the communities don't perceive it that way.

One of the goals of a place like the Justice Center in Red Hook is to address this issue of role of law and legal institutions and how the law interacts with citizens to produce public safety by creating a court that is physically closer to the community. A court that is more responsive to the community's problems, those problems that give rise to crime.

By becoming more accountable to communities, one justice center offers the possibility of a transformative role for the center and a court that will involve citizens in the processes of social regulation and control, which are essential to crime prevention. In other words, they are going to leverage legitimacy into public safety.

We have enormous amounts of data. Victoria has been in the field working with the court and living with the citizens of Red Hook for many months, and we are analyzing our data now. But one of the things that we're trying to do is to create a theoretical framework. We had a framework going into the study, and we're refining it and developing it now as we begin to look at the data.

So our talk is really more about theorizing about community justice and what works, and theorizing justice is something that I think is probably important to do. Why? Because if it's going to work here, we want to understand and explain why it's going to work somewhere else--that's the simplest question--and, second, we want to be able to give a good causal narrative, a good account.

In this theoretical perspective, the courts are part of a larger social network comprising the court and civil society, the community residents, all of which are working towards some kind of common good in the community.

The final goal of this partnership is that the court becomes an effective social institution that is grounded in that community, as opposed to being grounded in the centralized system downtown, and that it is going to engender more efficient mechanisms for addressing crime problems as they occur on the ground, both through formal mechanisms of justice and punishment and informal mechanisms of treatment, and also by again getting the citizens involved.

Conceptually, our justice center tries to do this in four specific ways. One, they deal with the social sources of crime. They try to have substantive impacts on criminal behavior through treatment and other remedial services, effective punishments, quick responses to wrongdoing, et cetera, et cetera.

Second, the court can build as a social agency, as well as a legal institution. It can build legitimacy because of the accretion of positive experiences of individuals who go through the court and who use the building. This court again signals the existence of a responsive process, a procedurally fair process. It has elements of therapeutic jurisprudence built in, community service.

66

All of this is communicated to the community at large through both the direct experience of the citizens in the court and also by some vicarious knowledge that they get because their neighbors are having contact with the court and going through the court and maybe even using the court. So we think, ultimately, there really is a process of contagion of thought and ideas and norms.

We think the court, again by its very presence, sends a signal that certain behaviors will not be tolerated. The law and the legal institution are part of the community, and those behaviors are rejected by the community. So again, there is this declarative effect of the presence of the court in the community.

Finally, what we think may be the most important result, is the creation of partnerships within the community, again either through these formal mechanisms of community groups, advisory boards, or informal mechanisms because of the individual relationships are built, all of them integrated within the local geography of the neighborhood. In other words, accountability via concrete forms of integration of citizens into the functioning of the law; a form of privatization of the law, which is something that there is pretty good empirical data tending to show that such privatization helps to build social control.

All of these mechanisms are pathways to legitimacy, and we think that legitimacy is ultimately what is going to leverage the court into social control, moving the court from being simply a legal institution into one that also helps to facilitate social control.

In the interest of time, let me talk about what we have seen so far as very concrete challenges to legitimacy, the kinds of problems that I think are illustrative of what community institutions like the justice center are going to face over time.

First, what bugs residents about crime in their neighborhoods are not the kinds of low-level misdemeanors and petty drug crimes that are coming through the court. What bugs them are robberies, gunshots, drug-selling, and high-level obnoxious drug selling.

The court is doing a nice job at bringing people in and dealing with the low-level misdemeanor issues, but it is not getting at the public safety issues, and people ultimately will look for a payoff down the road.

Second, it is not clear that people want therapeutic jurisprudence. What citizens and communities often complain about is being treated poorly by the courts, being treated unfairly. Sometimes we hear expressions in interviews with residents in the neighborhoods that what they want is more efficient case processing and fairer judgments, not necessarily to be treated or simply to have their problems diagnosed. They basically want the court to do justice, perhaps not necessarily treatment.

This is a very delicate balance that the court is treading on because, on the one hand, they do want to do good, and they have a hard job, and they are accomplishing a lot with their treatment interventions, but it is not necessarily what everybody wants.

And so, if there is a change in due process--in other words, the rights issue, which is sort of looming in the background of this whole symposium--it could very easily delegitimate the court in a way that the benefit to the common good is lost, because the loss of traditional roles means that the players cannot fulfill some of the expectations that the citizens actually have of the court, again a very delicate balance.

Third, the courts are just one player in the criminal justice system, and in places like Red Hook, the police are the biggest player. Some people in New York have lots of negative experiences with the police, others have positive experiences with the police, and the community still sees crime-solving as the responsibility of the police more so than the responsibility of the court.

It is not enough really for the court to say, "Well, the police are some externality, and we really can't deal with them; they are accountable down at Center Street, One Police Plaza, and so on." That will not work. There is going to have to be some concrete integration of the police into this creation of a new legal process within the community. It is part of that mechanism of accountability and privatization of social control that we talk about.

Fourth, Red Hook residents are constantly talking about their disillusionment with government and with the parts of governments that probably would make a very immediate and material difference in their lives--police and housing. Red Hook is eighty percent public housing, so there is some pressure on them to bring housing in. Now, the court is opening a housing part, but that would raise another very simple concrete example of a conflict.

The court is going to have a lot of drug defendants, and does have a lot of drug defendants, but when the housing part opens, there probably are going to be a lot of those same drug defendants who may well be evicted from public housing because of some of the laws and policies that are in effect both nationally and also in New York City. There is a very complicated, delicate balance for the court to tread. This will impose a legitimacy cost.

The major challenge that faces a community justice center and the efforts like it are to enlist the community in the creation of an undercurrent of a dynamic of legitimacy about the law, legal institutions, and in part about government programs in the

68

community. Through this legitimacy citizens become engaged in crime control and become engaged in social regulation.

Everybody in Criminal Law 102--not Criminal Law 101, but in Criminal Law 102--knows that you get a public safety payoff when there is interaction of formal and informal mechanisms of social control. That means the police and the citizens integrated together.

I think that is in large part what the Red Hook court and the Justice Center are trying to do, and there are two really bottom-line theoretical perspectives. The normative one is this: They are trying to leverage legitimacy into social control, and that is a good thing, and we are very happy to be able to be close to the ground and study how this process works and what challenges it faces.

But there is an economic theory and it is a simple one: Does the tradeoff pay off? Does the abrogation of rights pay off in terms of either better treatment within the court or better public safety and a better quality of life in the community outside the court? Because when you move into the community, you become just another government program, and hopefully, this one will work very well.

Barbara Babb University of Baltimore Law School
I am going to be talking about a court that is a little bit different than the kinds of courts you have heard about over the last day and most of this morning. I am going to be talking about a unified family court as a type of problem-solving court, and I have developed a theoretical framework for unified family courts that applies notions of therapeutic jurisprudence and the ecology of human development.

You heard yesterday about therapeutic jurisprudence. The ecology of human development is a social science systems theory that was developed by Professor Urie Bronfrenbrenner from Cornell University. Most of you may not have heard of him, but you probably have heard of Head Start. His research was responsible for initiating Head Start.

The unified family court that I propose is really a way to resolve the overwhelming volume and scope of family law matters in this country. I would like to give you just a little overview of my presentation. I am going to define a unified family court for you; give you a brief sense of the background and history of unified family courts, since they are different from drug treatment courts; talk a little bit about my framework; and then describe an example of a problem-solving court with this framework, which is the Maryland Family Division.

I want to read for you before I go further, if I can find things here, the mission statement that has been adopted by the court system in Maryland to define the work of our family divisions:

The mission of Maryland's family divisions is to provide a fair and efficient forum to resolve family legal matters in a problem-solving manner, with the goal of improving the lives of families and children who appear before the Court. To that end, the Court shall make appropriate services available for families who need them. The Court also shall provide an environment that supports judges, court staff, and attorneys so that they can respond effectively to the many legal and non-legal issues of families in the justice system.

I think that mission statement really incorporates a lot of what we've been talking about for the last day, and that mission statement is supported by thirteen core values of the family justice system in Maryland. I will talk a little bit more about this later.

Let me begin by talking about what is a unified family court. It really is a court with no agreed meaning, but I have been able to extract a few identifiers.

It is single court system with comprehensive subject matter jurisdiction. In order for this court to provide holistic treatment to families and children, the subject matter jurisdiction of the court has to be as comprehensive as possible, and by that we mean including everything related to family law matters: domestic violence, juvenile delinquency, child abuse and neglect, divorce, custody, child support, the full range of family law proceedings, including some inter-family offenses.

We are interested in having specially trained and interested judges. It's a court that addresses the legal, social, and emotional issues by affording families holistic treatment.

It's a court where informal court processes, social services, and resources are brought to bear for the families, either provided by the court or connected from the community to the court. We don't expect that the court can do everything for families, but it can make the connections back to the communities for the resources the families need.

It's a court that provides a comprehensive resolution to the families' legal matters instead of chipping away one issue at a time.

It is tailored to the individual family's legal, personal, emotional, and social needs. It must be tailored to the unique needs of that particular family. And it's a family that appears before one judge for one case or one judge for one family. In other words, we believe in continuity, that it is important for the family to not have to tell their story so many times, so that one judge who hears the beginning of the case should have to stay through that case until the end, and in some jurisdictions, every time the family comes back to court, they go before the same judge. It is a court that dispenses efficiency and compassion.

70

To give you just a brief history of the unified family courts, they are originally an outgrowth of the juvenile court movement. In 1899 the first juvenile court appeared. The first family court appeared in Cincinnati, Ohio, in 1914 and then a few selected cities. So while family court has been around since 1914, it really did not grow in popularity until the early 1960s. Rhode Island established the first family court in 1961; Hawaii followed in 1965; and New York, as many of you know, has a family court that was established in 1962.

Today, based on my most recent research, fourteen states have statewide family courts, which means that their entire state has a family court somewhere in the state where it is statewide. Twenty states have family courts in selected areas of the state. Maryland would fall into this category. It is generally situated in the areas of highest population.

Four states are planning family courts or are in the pilot stage, and thirteen states have no particular system for adjudicating family law matters; family court matters are mixed in with the rest of the civil docket.

Why is there a renewed interest in the family court concept today? Well, as you have heard, there are many problems with the existing court system. It is time-consuming, expensive, cumbersome, and duplicative. The same family can have to tell their story in many different courts or divisions of courts over and over, which is a waste of time and resources.

Child-related issues do not receive proper attention. Custody cases are often left to linger much longer than they should, rather than being given immediate attention. There is inadequate resort to alternative dispute resolution.

There is inadequate coordination of litigation involving the same family. As I said, the same family could find itself in several different courts depending on their legal issues, all of which are family law-related, or in different divisions of the same court.

There is a lack of interest, temperament, or understanding by some judges hearing family law cases, and this is particularly important in family law. If you do not want to be a family law judge, you should not be sitting in family court. These are cases which require that the litigants get the judge's attention and compassion and dedication to their issues.

And finally--and this is true, of course, across the nation-- there is a lack of attention to the needs of poor and unrepresented litigants.

To give you a context for considering these problems, family law cases are increasing in volume nationwide. They comprise thirty-five percent of the total civil filings nationwide, and they are increasing at a rate of 1.5 percent annually. They are the fastest growing portion of the civil trial docket.

In Maryland, family law cases, excluding juvenile delinquency and child abuse and neglect, constitute over fifty percent of our civil filings. If we added in juvenile delinquency and child abuse and neglect, that number would be much higher.

When you add to the extensive volume of these cases their complex scope, the fact that these cases involve some of the most intimate aspects of people's lives, and that they are often complicated by other issues such as substance abuse and domestic violence, it is an almost overwhelming task for the justice system to try to resolve these families' problems.

With regard to my interdisciplinary framework--I will talk about this briefly--I have created a blueprint to establish unified family courts. Not all of the family courts that I've talked about have this same type of family court setup, and part of the work that the center does that is relatively new. We are a resource to state justice systems; we provide research, technical assistance, and advocacy for states that are experimenting with their family justice systems and attempting to develop unified family courts or are trying to reform the way they currently handle family law matters. We do that through the application of therapeutic jurisprudence and the ecology of human development.

This is the blueprint that I've created to establish a family court. To go through this quickly, the court structure is specialized and separate. That doesn't mean that it has to be--it can be a division of an existing court, so that suffices. That is the way Maryland has structured its court system. It's a separate division of our trial court of general jurisdiction with specialized judges.

Now, I would advocate, as would most people who work in this field, that family law belongs at the same level as all other trial matters, so that the family court, whatever it is called, should be at the trial court of general jurisdiction.

I've already mentioned comprehensive subject matter jurisdiction. This affords the families holistic treatment.

Specialized case management. We believe in very early and hands-on case processing. It's an opportunity to link the families with the needed services very early on in the court process. It's an ongoing process. I've already mentioned the one judge-one case, one judge-one family approach.

Another approach is to have a consistent team of court personnel, including case managers, so that every time the family comes to court, they meet with members of the same team.

This creates a greater sense of the court with regard to its responsibility to families. It offers the court the opportunity to fashion more effective legal outcomes. But it does require a high degree of court administration and organization. So case-processing and case-management systems are very critical in our attempt to deliver this kind of justice.

The services, as I mentioned, can be either court-supplied or court-connected. Family courts are a wonderful way for the court to reach out to the community. What we've done in Maryland is create the position of family services coordinator in every jurisdiction. Part of that person's job is to assess all of the services that exist in the jurisdiction and bring available services to the court's attention so that we can link the court with those services, and judges have those resources available to them.

You do need to determine the essential services for your client population. So what is helpful in Baltimore City may not be helpful on the Eastern Shore or in Western Maryland, and these services should be delivered at the earliest possible point.

Finally, it has got to be a user-friendly court that is accessible to all litigants and accommodates litigants in the most therapeutic way possible. Probably ninety percent of the family law litigants in Baltimore City are unrepresented, so we struggle daily with ways to deliver justice to that unrepresented population, which is a major challenge.

That's the blueprint. The interdisciplinary framework I developed, as I said, incorporates both therapeutic jurisprudence and the ecology of human development. You heard yesterday from one of the founders of therapeutic jurisprudence what it is. I can't begin to top that, but I will tell you that, taking his cue, this is a court that is grounded in therapeutic jurisprudence, as he recommended, and it works. I can tell you that it is working.

How does it contribute to court reform in family law? Well, what's very important and central to family law decision-making with regard to therapeutic jurisprudence is that what constitutes a therapeutic outcome derives from the individual's own viewpoint. It is very individualized. The court has to determine what that is, assess it, and honor it. This is so important where you are dealing with intimate problems of people's lives.

I would suggest that by adopting a therapeutic approach in family law decision-making, you can and should expect the following consequences, and these are wonderful consequences for problem-solving courts and ought to be outcomes that other problem-solving courts should expect.

You empower individuals by allowing them to learn self-determining behavior and thereby, particularly in the family law context, decreasing the number of returns to court for the same family. They begin to learn to solve their own problems because the court itself is modeling problem-solving techniques for the litigants.

It is a wonderful way to empower judges, because it allows them to be creative and consider alternatives; yet it minimizes the abuse of their measures.

The central goal of all family law decision-making is to protect families and children from present and future harms. Therapeutic jurisprudence allows this to happen.

It decreases emotional turmoil and promotes family harmony or preservation. And we encourage a therapeutic role for all court personnel--the clerks, the facilitators, the case managers, even the sheriffs who stand at the metal detectors as you come in the door.

We had some visitors to our new Family Division in Baltimore City who recently commented about how wonderful it was to walk through the metal detectors where court personnel are actually happy and welcome you, and what a great thing for children who are having to come to the court system to be welcomed by men who are smiling and kind to them. We hope to encourage this environment and role for everyone.

And it provides individualized, efficient, and effective justice that is based on the needs of the parties.

I am not going to talk to you about the ecology of human development. But it is a systems theory, and it does allow judges and court personnel the ability, by application of this theory, to adopt a holistic approach to families and children.

I also believe, and this is just sort of the next piece that I am working on, that these two theories together can promote an ethic of care in the family justice system, and I think this ethic of care has to transcend everything that we do.

I want to talk about the Maryland courts that have been structured along these lines. We have an extensive list of services that we have developed in the Family Division in Baltimore City that are replicated in other divisions throughout our state. These are based on needs assessments, canvassing resources, building coalitions, and evaluating the initiatives.

We are evaluating our family divisions along the lines of trial court performance standards that have been developed by the Bureau of Justice Assistance. Courts really are evaluated differently. They are evaluated along five components: access to justice; expedition and timeliness; equality, fairness, and integrity; independence and accountability; and public trust and confidence.

What we are now attempting to do, at least those of us who work with the unified family courts, is to develop performance measures and standards so that courts can assess their own performance along these five measures.

My colleague, Jeff Kuhn and I recently worked with the State of Maryland, and actually, Judy Moran was involved in this study in its early stages, developing performance standards and measures for Maryland's family divisions. We worked with a group of judges, lawyers, and court personnel for over a year to together agree on what the performance measures should be.

We articulated the standard. We talked about issues related to the standard, and practical recommendations. Then we developed measurement systems to assess the outcomes, so that the courts can actually assess their own behavior.

The General Assembly in Maryland is very interested in this because they have funded the family divisions, at the insistence of our chief judge, Chief Judge Robert Bell, who is very supportive, and I do advocate judicial leadership from the top. Otherwise, this kind of law-reform effort is not going to succeed. I know this because I worked for ten years trying to make it happen in Maryland without the leadership of the chief judge. Once we got a new chief judge who said, "This just makes so much sense," my world turned around.

I am going to stop, but I will tell you that it's a wonderful and very worthwhile investment of time and energy because courts are the place that either everyone comes to or the problems find their way to, and it is really our responsibility as a society to try to help the litigants who come before the family justice system.

QUESTIONS AND ANSWERS

QUESTION: I have what I think is really a comment based on Adele Harrell's presentation. Adele showed us how what she described as contingency contracting is very important in increasing the satisfaction of the individual in drug treatment court.

I want to relate that--and this is a therapeutic jurisprudence point--to a body of social science research that I think shows how those of us in drug treatment court and in all of the problem-solving courts can kind of use this research in what we do.

I am referring to some work done in the mental health law area by the MacArthur network on mental health and the law, work done by John Monahan of the University of Virginia and his colleagues.

What they probed was the impact of coercion in the context of civil commitment. Mental hospitalization, when is coercion appropriate, does it work, and is it legally okay. They were looking at the question of whether involuntary treatment works compared to voluntary treatment, which is a burning issue in mental health law.

One would think you would look at involuntary commitment and compare it to voluntary commitment. But in truth, you cannot do that without having a thorough understanding of what makes people feel coerced, because what the MacArthur folks found was that being in one or another of those categories didn't really matter. People who were voluntarily admitted felt coerced--many of them did--and many people who were involuntarily committed, felt they made a voluntary decision.

So they did a study on the causes of these feelings and correlated them to what makes people feel coerced. What they found was that if people are given a sense of voice and validation and treated with dignity and respect and in good faith, then they feel uncoerced, even in a situation where they're subjected to legal compulsion.

Now let me relate this to what Ms. Harrell's presentation stated about contingency contracting. It seems to me that the point at which the individual enters into the contingency contract--this is a behavioral contract. This is the contract that the individual, in effect, does at the point at which they're entering drug treatment court, negotiating, in a way, with the judge as to the conditions.

I think we should make much more of that process. I think it should be a bit of a negotiation, a give-and-take. It's an opportunity for that individual to have a sense of voice and validation, dignity, and respect. It's an opportunity for the individual to feel, in other words, that the choice that he or she makes is a voluntary one. It's an opportunity for intrinsic motivation to kick in. It's an opportunity for motivation to be sparked.

So I would say that the judge and the lawyers should place a lot of emphasis on this point in the process and remind the individual from time to time during the process that that was the deal that he or she made.

This also relates to a body of largely theoretical psychological research that shows that people who feel uncoerced, who feel they have made voluntary choices, do much better, perform much better, than people who feel that they've been coerced, for whom there is often a bit of psychological reactants.

Anyway, this is simply a comment, not so much a question, but of course, if any of the panelists have any thoughts on this, I would love to hear about it.

MS. HARRELL: I am very curious myself for Jeff to reflect maybe on how this process of contingency contracting might play out in terms of legitimacy, because I think he put his finger on one of the central problems we have here.

MR. FAGAN: Well, it took me a long time to get very old, and so I was comfortable saying, "I have no idea." On the other hand, that never stopped me from speculating.

You know, I think there are two, there are three sides--the way I think about legitimacy, we think about three sides of it. One is sort of a bottom-line payoff. If it really does have a material improvement, then there is some kind of an economic payback.

There is a procedural part of it, an affective component: If it feels good, then people will see it as being a good process. It may turn out to be awful. There's a hypothetical I give students sometimes; suppose you were in a racial profiling context, and we just simply profiled the hell out of some population, but we all gave them pieces of candy afterwards and cards that said, "Well, I'm doing this because it's really in our own good." We violated the civil rights, but we make them feel good. So would people accept that or not?

But then the third is a distributive component, which is fairness. You know, is it done with fairness, is it done proportionally? Am I treated the same way that the guy next to me is treated? Are things proportional? Is the onerousness of the conditions that one's compliance or violation of the contract would evoke, is the response proportionate, and does that make sense to me in terms of what I did?

I think people have sort of an instinctual idea about what proportionality means and what the going rate should be for their violation.

So if you can pull it off that way, then I think you can, as a product of that dynamic, create a sense of legitimacy among people.

QUESTION: One of the things that Jeff raised in his initial look at what's going on in Red Hook is that it's not clear that the community wants therapeutic justice, and they may want fairness and efficiency more.

I am wondering the extent to which we are using problem-solving courts or developing methods of therapeutic jurisprudence as a substitute for providing the traditional mechanisms that we look at as fairness, like lawyers for the litigants, because we haven't solved that problem. So how much does that impact on the decision to take another route because the other route might help us to solve that problem?

MS. BABB: I don't think that problem-solving courts or a problem-solving approach grew out of a frustration about what to do with unrepresented litigants. I think judges, litigants, the community at large, essentially everyone was discouraged about how family law matters had been handled. I will speak about those because that is what I do and that is what I study. So I think it was really a need where nobody was satisfied, and nobody was really being helped.

What happened to me was backing into this notion of therapeutic jurisprudence and saying, "This is exactly the way I practice law, and wouldn't it be great if we could really sort of transform people's attitudes about how to resolve family legal problems?" They are legal problems. Why not apply a problem-solving approach? Why not look at it as the court's responsibility to help the people who are there.

The court will have some effect no matter what it does, so why not change the focus from being a sort of a blank slate to one where they actively look for a way to help the families and children that are before the court?

I don't think that the increasing number of pro se litigants contributed to this, but I think in many ways pro se litigants are better served by this kind of court system because even though they don't have lawyers, they have resources available to them. We have made great strides in making the court system accessible to pro se litigants by developing form pleadings so that they now have access to justice, of which they had none in the past, and some services.

So there are places along the process where they are actually being better served by this.

MS. HARRELL: What I have encountered in doing focus groups is that most people coming through, even if they have an appointed defense counsel, don't understand the rules, don't feel represented, don't feel like they have a voice, and don't understand what is going to happen to them.

So to the extent that this resolves some of those problems, they may feel better served by this process.

QUESTION: As most of you know, especially New Yorkers in the audience, Chief Judge Kaye is vigorously promoting a restructuring of the court system here in New York State, which heretofore has been very fractured by eleven different ways of getting into the justice system at the trial level.

I am wondering if any of the panelists could comment on what effect restructuring New York's court system to make one trial-level court with divisions for families, and criminal, and civil, would have on the problem-solving model. Would it enhance it? Would we do away with it?

78

MS. BABB: I am happy to respond to that. I practiced law in New York for three years. Passing the New York Bar and learning about all the different courts is a pain.

While New York has a family court, that court doesn't have jurisdiction over divorce. So it doesn't have comprehensive subject-matter jurisdiction. It has many wonderful features, but it doesn't have the ability to treat the family holistically.

I think it certainly would benefit the citizens of New York to try to consolidate some of those courts. I practiced law in someone's kitchen in Upstate New York. Court was actually held in her kitchen with the dishwasher running. I'm not sure--that was not my notion of justice.

QUESTION: One of the things that has struck me as I have studied problem-solving courts is the following tension--I won't quite say "contradiction"--that I thought you might shed some light on, which is there is a lot of--one of the buzzwords is "holistic approach," right? Someone comes in, there's a family problem, it's a juvenile problem, there's a custody problem, whatever it is, and you say, "Well, we want to treat the whole family together." All right.

But, alternatively, you could say, "Well, part of this family problem is a drug problem." So when you say a holistic approach, what one immediately thinks is, well, there ought to be a court with sort of comprehensive jurisdiction to decide everything because, of course, all social problems are interconnected.

And yet the movement has generally been to establish specialized courts of relatively broad jurisdiction within a certain specialty.

My question is--it is more a puzzlement--as to how one decides in the first instance whether a constellation of problems that has a housing component, that has a drug-addiction component, that has a family component, gets diverted to one of these courts and whether there is any thinking about comprehensively what the appropriate units are, without then giving up on this sort of holism.

MS. BABB: I think that one reason to concentrate on unified family courts is given the extensive volume of cases that they occupy in the justice system, I mean, to me that's a natural, that's a start.

I think that the scope of those cases is extensive enough already--and I've seen some of the issues in terms of trying to get specialized judges and services delivered to those families--that I would be opposed to broadening that jurisdiction much more. I think it's very effective as a way to resolve families' legal problems.

I do have some concerns about some of the spin-off specialized courts that come out of a unified family court, and I think there we are starting down the same path to--you know, we have the potential to give conflicting orders, duplicative proceedings, so that I have some concerns about that. But I think that the family piece of it is a large enough chunk to be self-contained.

MS. HARRELL: I have real concerns about the drug court specialties and the narrowness of eligibility rules for some drug courts that begin to shut out and perhaps focus all the resources on the less needy cases, because they've got mental health problems or they're not citizens and cannot qualify for publicly funded treatment or have a history of violence.

These may be the very people that are most deserving of these resources, not least.

MR. REMPEL: In essence, some of the community courts, the Red Hook Community Justice Center, are really what you're describing in a sense in that they're a single court that is really attempting to address a multiplicity of problems in terms of housing, substance abuse, unemployment, and educational component.

Though of course, the community courts, what is limiting about them is that, at least in the New York City example, they just had to take your "low-level" misdemeanor cases, so that you don't currently have a comprehensive court for all levels of charges that address all levels of problems.

We already have a model in the community courts that one could look to if one wanted to expand in that direction, and it may be inevitable that the more holistic problem-solving court that you suggest will occur at some point. I think it's just in some sense an evolutionary process that you've anticipated.

MR. FAGAN: Well, in Red Hook there are separate parts, and there are separate judges sitting in the separate parts. But he's handling separate problems separately, right, in separate callings. So it's kind of an optimization strategy, right? And it's a gamble because I am not sure--if the accountability mechanism is back through this process, then the optimization strategy is great, and one hopes for the right payoffs.

It requires a very special kind of judge to be able to do that, I think, to have substantive knowledge about the law in very diverse areas, and sometimes very complicated problems.

I think, just before you came in, we raised this tension about a drug defendant walking in, a person on a drug charge, and is dealing with a drug charge on one docket, and on another docket they are going to evict the kid, the guy's mother from public housing, and I am not sure how you optimize that one. That is just one example of--you could see the same issues around--so, for example, in the Nicholson case, the Supreme Court case on removal of children from ACS, there are tensions, and I am not sure what the optimization is there, either.

Nicholson is a case in federal court in Brooklyn, a class action of battered women whose children were removed by the child welfare agency to protect the children and avoid their exposure to violence and danger. But still, there is this tension about how you resolve that kind of matter.

It is an evolution. I am not sure how it's going to evolve. It's a real challenge.

QUESTION: I just wanted to comment on the last set of thoughts about creating a comprehensive community model. Having studied the problem-solving court movement, there is a question that has come up throughout its sort of later stages of development over the last couple of years, and the question is, How does the problem-solving court movement go to scale?

The question is, Are we in the court system developing these experiments within certain areas where we feel a therapeutic jurisprudence approach or a different administrative approach is going to yield different results, and we are creating these experiments like drug courts and community courts, and we are then going to take those experiments and apply the lessons to a larger court system like Adele has discussed in the research that she has done on creating a comprehensive model where, for instance, any offense that has a drug-related component would result in some sort of treatment disposition?

Or is that we are just creating, magnifying these specialized courts? You know, you hear the numbers that people described, that in the year 2000 there were 500 drug courts, and now there are close to 1000. Is it that we want to multiply these specialty areas, or do we want to bring them back to the larger court system?

I guess that starts as a comment and goes to a question to the panel. What do the panelists think about that going-to-scale question?

And in terms of the notion of a comprehensive court, a sort of different idea of going to scale is that we've concentrated a great deal of attention in the court system on unifying the court system and creating centralized models to avoid local corruption; and now we are looking at the idea that that is an alienating model in terms of delivering justice in an efficient way. And so we are looking at actually putting the courts back into communities and experimenting with that as a model to create a comprehensive structure. So again, there is another going-to-scale question that the community courts raise.

So I guess my question cuts across all of your presentations to ask, you know, how do you see that going-to-scale question operating in problem-solving courts?

MS. HARRELL: I can talk about breaking the cycle, and that's the program that you referred to, and it's an attempt to take--it's a demonstration project that is essentially testing the feasibility of taking a drug court kind of concept but separating it from a problem-solving court concept to simply saying that every justice agency would make appropriate treatment referrals for drug-involved offenders independently of case processing. So if they were sentenced to jail, they would get it there; if they were sentenced to prison, they would get it there; if they were put on probation, they would get it there if they wanted community release.

The way the program--it's now in its, what, fourth year of evaluation?--is playing out is that what the communities involved have chosen to do is to not use a drug court model, but they are very much incorporating treatment alternatives in lieu of incarceration. So I think to that extent what they have done is take the concept of therapy but not link it as tightly to the processing of the case.

QUESTION: I was just going to say that within the idea of a community court, I think what we were trying to say is that a community court has to be more than just an efficient service provider, which is what a lot of the problem-solving courts that we've been discussing, like drug courts, are essentially on many levels aiming to be, that a community court has to somehow engage the community, which I don't think could happen from a central court system, and a community court--I mean, the idea of it is the community itself wants more than just services. I mean, it wants some type of role within the court system.

I don't think that that sort of model can be taken to scale. But being an efficient service provider is something that the system should be at this point.

3

Problem-Solving Courts: From Innovation to Institutionalization

Michael C. Dorf; Jeffrey Fagan

The phenomenal growth of drug courts and other forms of "problem-solving" courts has followed a pattern that is characteristic of many successful innovations: An individual or small group has or stumbles upon a new idea; the idea is put into practice and appears to work; a small number of other actors adopt the innovation and have similar experiences; if there is great demand for the innovation--for example, because it responds to a widely-perceived crisis or satisfies an institutional need and resolves tensions within organizations that adopt it--the innovation rapidly diffuses through the networks in which the early adopters interact. Eventually, what was originally an innovation becomes institutionalized.

Three institutional imperatives gave rise to the diffusion of drug courts. First was the docket pressure created by intensification of the war on drugs in the 1980s. Second was the perception shared by the public and legal elites that the crash of drag cases led to a crisis in the courts, characterized by an ineffective system of punishment and a "revolving door" that recycled offenders without reducing either their drag use or criminality. Third was discomfort among some trial court judges with the restricted sentencing discretion in drag laws enacted during this same period, creating incentives for experimentation with sentencing alternatives. At the same time, the popular demand for punitive responses to control what was perceived as a runaway epidemic of drags and collateral social problems focused the courts on solutions that blended judicial control with therapeutic interventions.

Problem-solving courts: From innovation to institutionalization, by Michael C. Dorf and Jeffrey Fagan (2003). American Criminal Law and Review, Fall 2003 v40 i4, p1501 (11). Reprinted by permission. Endnotes have been removed.

Drug courts provided a structure and philosophy that promised to resolve each of these tensions. Whereas the public at large tended to view drug-addicted criminals chiefly as a social menace, judges and other legal actors were more comfortable treating (nonviolent) offenses committed by drag addicts as a medical problem. Indeed, because drug courts emphasized both the individual responsibility of drug addicts and the disease model of addiction, they enabled persons with widely divergent views about drug policy to find common ground. They were, in short, an innovation well suited to the times.

After nearly a decade and a half of experimentation and diffusion, problem-solving courts are quickly reaching the institutionalization phase of their relatively brief natural history. The progenitor of modern drug courts first opened in Miami in 1989 and included Janet Reno among its key participants. As Attorney General through both of President Clinton's terms, Reno would provide seed money for drug courts nationwide. The seeds took root. As of October 2003, there were 1,091 operating drug courts, with another 413 in the planning stage. Many of the original drug court innovators have moved on to other endeavors, and a new generation of actors is quickly replacing them. Professionalization and standardization have grown as innovation has begun to give way to institutionalization.

Accordingly, problem-solving courts are now at a critical turning point, presenting a fitting moment to pose a series of policy and practical questions reflecting the issues that have emerged since their inception. To that end, lawyers, judges and scholars specializing in law and social science gathered at Columbia Law School in April 2003 to reflect on the experience of problem-solving and community courts, and to ask what comes next. The essays and commentaries in this Symposium reflect the wide range of reactions that problem-solving courts have sparked, and the issues that the next generation of actors in problem-solving courts will face.

Candace McCoy explores the evolution and growth of drug courts. She draws a cautionary lesson from other efforts at judicial reform--particularly the juvenile courts that emerged at the turn of the twentieth century and the movement from indeterminate to determinate sentencing that took hold in the 1980s. Both phenomena are closely related to modern problem-solving courts. The juvenile courts were for a long time rationalized as therapeutic rather than retributivist interventions in the lives of young offenders, just as problem-solving courts have been rationalized as practicing therapeutic justice. Both reforms sought to avoid the potential harms of formal punishment. Moreover, both drug courts and juvenile courts shared an optimism about the promise of rehabilitation, drew service providers into the influence (if not control) of the court, and used the legal authority of the court to direct offenders to therapeutic interventions rather than punitive sentences.

The similarities between the evolution of determinate sentencing and the history of the drug court movement are even more direct: Sentencing guidelines that imposed stiff mandatory penalties (for drug offenses, among others) led to overcrowded prisons and dockets; this generated pressure to divert cases from the courts, which led in turn to the renewed political viability of measures, such as drug courts, that were not strictly punitive. But just as the determinate sentencing movement, which began with bipartisan consensus, quickly became a vehicle for those who simply sought the harshest possible penalties, so McCoy warns that the left-right alliance that gave rise to drug courts could easily fall prey to politics. With federal money for crime control programs drying up and states facing grim fiscal crises, drug courts could become a hollow shell: starved of the resources to provide or monitor needed services, they would be unable to prove their worth. At the extreme, severely underfunded drug courts might end up doing more harm than good.

On the other hand, if drug courts do receive sufficient resources, McCoy's analysis suggests a different danger. She notes that many of the champions of drug courts view them as a means of circumventing what they regard as unduly harsh mandatory minimum sentences. While we share McCoy's normative view of such sentences, we wonder how long drug courts can fly under the radar of the larger political debate. If the public demands harsh sentences, then a program that successfully circumvents popular demand for punishment seems politically vulnerable. In her commentary on Professor McCoy's paper, Laurie Robinson takes issue with the analogy to the political movement for determinate sentencing. Robinson notes that the problem-solving court movement has been a "grass-roots" phenomenon, about which national politicians have had little to say. The question that neither McCoy nor Robinson can answer is what will happen when the political spotlight does fall on problem-solving courts. The enthusiastic embrace of drug courts by trial court judges and recent endorsements from appellate courts provide a dramatic backdrop to the possibility of an unfolding tension between the judiciary and the political branches over the future of this reform.

Ultimately, the political future of drug courts and problem-solving courts more generally will depend upon their efficacy and cost-effectiveness as a response to crime. Efficacy and cost-effectiveness, of course, have long been the chief selling points of drug courts; yet, as both the defenders and critics of drug courts agree, most studies are inconclusive with respect to these criteria. Although none of the principal papers in this symposium directly addresses the efficacy question, several of the participants--including supporters Steven Belenko and Michael Rempel as well as critics Morris Hoffman and James Nolan--refer to issues of efficacy.

Our own view is cautious: we agree with the critics that many of the studies often invoked by drug court supporters are flawed, inconclusive or both. The main lesson we draw with respect to efficacy questions is that more, and better, research needs to be undertaken. Well-designed assignment schemes and long-term longitudinal studies that enable direct measurement of recidivism would go a long way toward answering the key questions. Encouragingly, the round of clinical trials and other controlled studies recently completed by drug courts and their supporters suggests that those in the field take this challenge seriously, too. The evidentiary bar is set high in these studies--which is to the good--and thus there are both large risks and large potential benefits for the "movement" in this development.

Beyond commissioning one-time studies, problem-solving courts could institutionalize a form of permanent self-study aimed at self-improvement. The information technology that permits drug courts to closely monitor defendants' performance in treatment should enable the courts to monitor their own performance. In the coming years, drug courts and those that study them should also be able to compare the performance of various treatment providers and modalities. Assuming that treatment is more efficacious than no treatment, under what circumstances does inpatient treatment outperform outpatient treatment? What is the ideal duration of treatment for a given type of addiction? To what extent can other drugs, such as methadone, play a part in treatment, and if they do, is permanent reliance on such drugs an acceptable outcome or just another form of addiction? How efficacious are treatment modalities that are expressly religious or quasi-religious (such as "twelve-step programs" that require submission to "a Higher Power"), and how does their effectiveness compare to programs that rely on secular systemic or psychological-therapeutic methods? In answering questions such as these, problem-solving courts will face a challenge in trying to provide answers based on solid research rather than ideology.

WHAT IS THE DOMAIN OF PROBLEM-SOLVING COURTS?

As problem-solving courts increasingly tackle problems besides drug addiction, efficacy questions become entangled with more directly normative concerns. No commentators have yet suggested a heuristic to decide which types of social problems and crimes are amenable to, or appropriate for, problem-solving courts, and what conditions must exist for courts to take this step. There are now specialized courts for mentally ill offenders, drunk drivers, parole or probation violators, gun carriers, domestic violence offenders, and several other types of offenses and offenders. Why these problems and not others?

Domestic violence courts, for example, were established before there was any known effective treatment for batterers. Moreover, as a normative matter, the very idea of "treating" someone for the propensity to commit acts of domestic violence may appear to excuse such acts of violence. There is likely to be enormous (and justified) political resistance to classifying such a propensity as a disease in the same way that drug courts accept the disease model of addiction--and that opposition would likely remain (and perhaps justifiably so) even if there were a scientific basis for the disease classification.

Even if one were willing to pathologize domestic violence as a form of mental illness, the heterogeneity among offenders further complicates both the scientific basis for therapeutic intervention and the normative question. Some assailants undoubtedly do manifest mental health abnormalities or disorders that would justify treatment in lieu of punishment or coupled with punishment. But many other assailants do not have these symptoms, and certainly would not merit a reduction in punishment. These tensions are not unique to domestic violence cases; the very idea of treatment for anyone who has violated the criminal law raises basic moral questions. But the issue is heightened in the case of domestic violence, where there is an identifiable and vulnerable victim, so that the system's failure in any given case creates an issue of not just public safety but the safety of a particular person.

Accordingly, whether and where domestic violence courts fit in the problem-solving-court model is one of many questions about the model itself. To some extent, problem-solving courts are simply specialized courts that develop expertise with particular problems. In this account, drug courts, domestic violence courts, mental health courts, and the like are criminal cousins of civil forums such as bankruptcy courts, tax courts, and the United States Court of Appeals for the Federal Circuit (which has exclusive jurisdiction over patent appeals). Beyond the obvious fact that the criminal problem-solving courts can threaten to, and in fact do, imprison people, what distinguishes them from other (civil) courts of specialized jurisdiction is their capacity to provide and/or monitor the provision of services that go beyond the particular jurisdictional hook that brings the parties into court in the first place. And, problem-solving courts create a web of reciprocal accountability between courts, defendants and treatment providers that transcends the traditional adversarial roles in both civil and criminal courts.

Is the ability to integrate services holistically the feature that unites the various kinds of courts under the problem-solving rubric? If so, we face a puzzle, for increased specialization--separate courts for drug addiction, housing disputes, mental health issues, domestic violence, and so forth--runs in the opposite direction of holistic jurisprudence. Indeed, "community courts" such as the Red Hook Community Justice Center in the Red Hook neighborhood of Brooklyn, New York, tout as one of their principal advantages their lack of specialization. The fact that the same judge hears cases falling within several jurisdictional categories, it is claimed, enables him to devise solutions that do not solve one problem only by exacerbating another. For example, federally assisted housing authorities take a zero-tolerance approach to drug possession, so that a conventional drug court judge might aid an addict in kicking the habit only at the cost of having him and his family evicted from their apartment; by contrast, a community court judge could, in principle, obtain the forbearance of the housing authorities for a resident receiving drug treatment so long as the resident remains under the judge's supervision.

Of course, a community court judge can only act across subject matter jurisdictional boundaries if she has control over her docket. Accordingly, community courts are necessarily small courts. That is, as Jane Spinak noted in a comment during the Symposium, one of their key advantages. But size has its advantages too. Due to its expansive case load, the Brooklyn Treatment Court (for drug-addicted offenders) is able to feed a large number of clients to many different service providers. It thus has the capacity to learn what programs are most effective and use the performance of the best providers as a standard against which to measure the others. Community courts serving smaller populations across subject-matter jurisdictional boundaries may be able to piggy-back on the information obtained by such larger courts--especially if they are geographically proximate, as in the case of Red Hook and the Brooklyn Treatment Court--but they cannot themselves develop large databases as effectively as the larger courts.

By calling attention to the wide variety of problem-solving courts, we do not mean to imply that the problem-solving court model is so capacious as to be vacuous. Relative to conventional courts, nearly all problem-solving courts are characterized by a problem orientation and closer monitoring of what takes place outside the courtroom. This, in turn, leads to a set of questions that are addressed in most of the principal papers in this Symposium. James Nolan asks whether the practice of therapeutic jurisprudence is consistent with the kind of independence and detachment traditionally thought essential for the judiciary to perform its distinctive function in a liberal democracy. William Simon asks whether defense attorneys can act consistently with their ethical duties when representing clients in drug courts and other problem-solving courts. And Victoria Malkin asks what role the community plays in defining the problems that problem-solving courts address and how the community is defined.

These are all urgent questions, and answering any of them completely requires an answer to the others. Simon, for example, confronts the complaint that problem-solving courts unacceptably place lawyers in the position of having to cooperate with the state. He notes that even in other settings the law frequently assigns defense attorneys duties to third parties and the court. He concludes that lawyers engaged in transactional work, rather than in litigation, may provide a better model for lawyering in problem-solving courts. Indeed, the "contracts" that many problem-solving courts require clients to sign call for just those lawyering skills in the defense attorney that one associates with the transactional attorney.

Moreover, Simon argues, problem-solving courts do not even pose a fundamental challenge to the traditional conception of the courtroom attorney. He observes that the standard conception of the lawyer as zealous advocate obligates the lawyer to pursue any lawful means of advancing her client's interest, but that nothing in that conception requires that the law define the bounds of permissible advocacy in a way that invariably favors defendants. In other words, if problem-solving courts provide defense attorneys with fewer mechanisms with which to advance their clients' interest in avoiding penal sanction, that poses no ethical dilemma, so long as the attorney takes advantage of the opportunities the law provides to address offenders' therapeutic needs.

Simon's answer perhaps suffices to dispatch the concerns of individual attorneys practicing in problem-solving courts, but it points to systemic concerns as well. >From the standpoint of institutional design, we want the law to provide defense attorneys with just those procedural rights that ensure a fair adjudicative process, nothing more and nothing less. Yet a therapeutic orientation, Nolan contends, deprives defendants and the system as a whole of a critical determinant of due process: a detached and neutral judge. When the state expressly advocates imprisonment as a means of retribution, incapacitation or deterrence, the judge understands that the interests of the state and of the defendant are antagonistic, and that the judicial function is to give each side a fair heating. However, when the state proposes treatment backed by threat of punishment for the defendant's own good, the judge may lose sight of the fact that interests remain opposed. As a result, the judge may--and Nolan shows that he sometimes does--pressure clients into treatment, acting, in effect, as just another coercive arm of the state by adopting principles of "harm reduction."

Although Nolan's criticisms suggest a fundamental incompatibility between justice and the consequentialism that underlies the drug court and problem-solving court approach, he does not, in the end, condemn drug courts and problem-solving courts outright. Rather, he intends his critique as an admonition to those who would institutionalize such courts to consider their impact on the traditional goals of the criminal justice system. That admonition can be taken in one of two ways. One might think, as we suspect Nolan himself does, that the costs to justice are too high and the returns to crime control and offenders are too low, and that the experiment with problem-solving courts ought to be abandoned. Alternatively, one might welcome problem-solving courts--or at least accept them as a fait accompli --and ask what measures can be taken to ensure that due process is appropriately reconceptualized and respected within such courts.

Due process is not the only area in which problem-solving courts could stand to improve. McCoy's paper shows that problem-solving courts arose from a movement of elites--principally judges. Yet if they are to be successful in the long term, and if they are to produce the normative legitimacy needed to leverage social control among their users, problem-solving courts must address the problems that affect the people whose communities they serve. And Malkin's paper indicates that, while institutions like the Red Hook Community Justice Center want to address community needs, there remains a gap between community perceptions of the problems that need addressing and the perceptions of the court personnel. How to close that gap--how to mediate between the technocratic logic of a problem-solving court and the democratic logic of a community court--remains one of the main challenges for problem-solving and community courts.

The pages that follow contain a wide range of thoughtful approaches to the questions we have flagged and many others. These richly nuanced essays will, we hope, spark further debate over a phenomenon that--for good or ill--can no longer be dismissed as a sideshow to the real action in traditional courts.

Michael C. Dorf and Jeffrey A. Fagan. The authors are, respectively, Professor of Law and Professor of Law and Public Health at Columbia University. They thank Tim Casey for service above and beyond the call of duty in organizing this Symposium, the editors and staff of the American Criminal Law Review for their hard work and patience, and Zachary Tripp for excellent research assistance.

Part 4

Incarcerated Women
and their Children

1

Attachment Disorders: Review and Current Status

Samantha L. Wilson

Author's Abstract

Developmental research on attachment has flourished in the past 15 years. However, there has been relatively scant empirical investigation of disorders in attachment. In this article, the pertinent developmental research on the attachment cycle is delineated and the current status of disordered attachment is examined. A particular focus is given to the conceptualization of the most severe form of disordered attachment, Reactive Attachment Disorder.

The infant-caregiver relationship has long been defined as crucial to later personality development. Attachment within this relationship has proven to be an interesting aspect of developmental research. Beginning with Bowlby's conceptualization of attachment, researchers have developed a more complete understanding of the attachment cycle and a greater appreciation of future implications when it is disrupted. However, we are far from a comprehensive understanding of attachment disorders--their behavioral manifestations, diagnoses, and treatments. To fully understand the current state of research in this area, I have examined the current status of disordered attachment.

Bowlby was one of the first researchers to suggest the importance of early relationships on the social and emotional development of children. His theory conceptualized attachment as a biological drive toward species survival. He theorized that selective attachment provided protection from predators. In doing so, he

Attachment Disorders: Review and Current Status (Jan 2001), by Samantha L. Wilson. The Journal of Psychology, v135 i1 p37 (15). Used by permission. References have been removed.

revolutionized thinking about a child's tie to a caregiver and its disruption throughout separation and deprivation. Bowlby divided the attachment cycle into four phases occurring during the first few years of life.

An infant exhibits certain cues during the first years of life that encourage proximity to a caregiver. Bowlby suggested that these represent a biological repertoire of signaling behaviors to induce individuals to approach, thus increasing proximity and physical contact. During the first phase of the attachment cycle, crying is the dominant signaling behavior. The cry of the infant signals the caregiver to provide relief for the child. In addition, Bowlby felt that the infant is equipped with additional behaviors (e.g., rooting, sucking, and grasping) in order to prolong the physical contact. These behaviors are the basis of attachment formation in that they seek to minimize distance between infant and caregiver. What separates the first phase of the attachment cycle from later phases is the nondiscriminatory manner in which these signaling behaviors are displayed.

Bowlby set the beginning of the second attachment phase at the onset of discrimination between figures and a marked preference for a common caregiver. This discrimination, which begins between 8 and 12 weeks of age, directs signaling behaviors toward a particular individual. During this phase the infant expands the seeking behaviors to include coordinated reaching and scooting.

Ainsworth, Blehar, Waters, and Wall cautioned that this preference for a caregiver is not necessarily indicative of attachment. They prefer to characterize the establishment of attachment as occurring during the third phase of Bowlby's attachment cycle. During this phase, the infant begins to actively pursue a preferred caregiver. An infant in this stage is said to rely more on active efforts to maintain proximity versus the passive signaling behaviors that dominate previous stages. Attachment during this phase is displayed through more active behaviors such as following a departing caregiver, greeting a returning caregiver, or seeking to be in closer proximity. Although active measures dominate this phase of the attachment cycle, signaling behaviors continue to be used as language begins to develop.

Bowlby considered the third phase to continue through the second birthday and to mark the beginning of "goal-corrected" behavior. That is, the infant begins to anticipate the caregiver's actions, given that these actions have a reasonable degree of consistency. Bowlby suggested that an infant in Phase 3 is capable of taking these expectations into account when organizing attachment behaviors. The infant then adjusts actions to a caregiver's anticipated behavior.

The fundamental feature of the fourth phase of the attachment cycle is the infant's understanding of the caregiver's independence. Here, the infant begins to acquire insight into the caregiver's motives and feelings. This characterizes the evolution of a partnership between infant and caregiver and an extension of the original bond into a more sophisticated form of attachment. Bowlby continued to define this phase as a organization of the infant's attachment behaviors and the caregiver's reciprocal behavior. Although Bowlby was specifically concerned with the attachment of infant to mother, he suggested that this model was useful for defining attachments to other figures.

Within this framework, attachment is conceptualized as an intense and enduring bond biologically rooted in the function of protection from danger. This is the evolutionary basis of attachment; however, it remains that attachment is a subjective experience of the infant based on a consistent alleviation of infant needs. The infant's biological needs and behavioral requests (in the form of crying or reaching) must be consistently answered by the caregiver in order to foster the sense of trust and security imperative for attachment to occur. If these needs are appropriately met, the caregiver becomes a conditioned source of comfort.

Bowlby believed that the infant uses these early experiences to develop an internal working model, later influencing interpersonal perceptions, attitudes, and expectations. If an infant is cared for consistently, the internal model will reflect that consistency, and trust will begin to form. The implication of this is that the infant will maintain normative social development given that the environment satisfies these biological needs consistently.

Ainsworth et al. expanded on Bowlby's original theory by contributing the notion of the caregiver as a secure base from which an infant explores surroundings. In addition, they introduced the concept of caregiver sensitivity to infant signals and the role of this sensitivity in the development of infant--caregiver attachment patterns. The concept of caregiver sensitivity addressed the problem of individual variation in attachment formation by declaring that a responsive, sensitive caregiver was of critical importance to the development of a secure, versus an insecure, attachment pattern.

THE STRANGE SITUATION

Ainsworth et al. were among the first to test these ideas empirically; they subsequently developed the most widely used research method for assessing the quality of attachment. This classification system is based on a 20-min laboratory procedure (the Strange Situation)

defining attachment patterns in terms of the infant's response to
reunion with the caregiver after two brief separations.

The original findings of Ainsworth et al. delineated three
distinct patterns of attachment behaviors. Infants within Group A
were labeled insecure/avoidant. These infants show a marked
avoidance of proximity to the caregiver in the reunion episodes. They
either ignore or casually greet the caregiver, mingling the welcome
with avoidance responses such as turning away from or moving past
the caregiver. These infants often show little distress at being
released from the caregiver's hold and tend to treat a stranger with a
response similar to that given the caregiver. Distress during the
separation may to be due to solitude rather than to the departure of
the caregiver, as the infant is easily consoled by the stranger.

Group B comprised infants characterized as secure. A
securely attached infant actively seeks physical contact with the
caregiver and resists release attempts. These infants are distinguished
from other groups by the fact that there is little sign of avoidance or
resistance to proximity with the caregiver. Signaling behaviors (i.e.,
reaching, scooting, and crying) are heightened on reunion with the
caregiver. However, during pre-separation episodes the infant is not
preoccupied with the caregiver's presence, but rather uses the
caregiver as a secure exploratory base. These infants show a marked
preference for the familiar caregiver over a stranger and are more
easily comforted by the caregiver.

The third group, Group C, was characterized as
insecure/resistant infants. These infants display noticeable resistance
to contact and interaction with the caregiver on reunion. They may
seek initial proximity to the caregiver only to reject it by pushing
away or squirming. These infants display more maladaptive behavior
patterns and tend to be angrier than infants in other groups.
Ambivalence and a lack of active exploratory behavior in the
presence of the caregivers is characteristic of this group.

Main and Solomon later identified a fourth group, Group D,
consisting of disorganized or disoriented infants. These infants
display no coherent pattern in their coping strategies during the
separation episodes. Their behavior appears to lack an observable
goal and tends to be contradictory. Movements are undirected,
misdirected, or interrupted. Also, these infants display behaviors
indicating confusion and apprehension toward the caregiver.

Although categories derived from the Strange Situation have
proven to be extremely useful in guiding attachment research, they
are not easily transferred to the clinical diagnosis of attachment
disorders. In other words, children classified as anxiously or
insecurely attached do not necessarily suffer from an attachment
disorder, but rather represent a graded continuum of attachment

problems. However, clinically significant attachment disturbances do represent a subgroup of insecurely attached infants. Thus, to be classified as a disorder, the infant's behavioral organization must severely impair functioning across several areas of life.

Boris et al. delineated numerous behaviors that should be assessed to determine whether a particular pattern of attachment is clinically significant. Primarily, the style of showing affection and seeking comfort from the caregiver should be observed. A lack of affectionate interchange between child and caregiver and/or indiscriminate affection with strangers is cause for concern. Another clinical area of behavior is the degree of cooperation between child and caregiver. Specifically, excessive dependence on the caregiver or an inability to seek the support of the attachment figure is problematic. Exploratory behaviors are of clinical interest as well. A child that fails to check back with the caregiver or use the caregiver as a secure exploratory base may be displaying disturbed attachment behaviors.

Boris et al. concluded that the clinical assessment of attachment disturbances should be based on a focused history and a systematic observation of parent/infant interaction. Together, these provide a clinician with the opportunity to highlight potential barriers to normative attachment development, including the physical or emotional unavailability of the caregiver due to illness, addiction, developmental disability, or extended separation.

These life events can be clinically significant in the formation of attachment patterns. For example, Bowlby first described the impact of infant/caregiver separation in his examination of institutionalized infants, in which he delineated three general phases observed on separation of the infant from the primary caregiver as protest, despair, and detachment. During the initial phase, the child displays obvious signs of distress: extensive crying, searching behavior, and refusal of alternative figures. Eventually the acting-out behaviors subside, and the child withdraws from social interaction. Seemingly in a state of mourning, the child becomes inactive and passive toward the environment. With time, the child moves to what Bowlby called the detachment phase. Here the child no longer rejects alternative figures, but upon reuniting with the original attachment figure, the child is apathetic and remote.

Along with extended separation, inconsistent care can disturb the formation of trust needed to form a lasting attachment bond. This may be due in part to the inability of the infant, caregiver, or both to fully understand how to relate to a person in an intimate or reciprocal manner. Therefore, the quality of the caregiver's emotional availability early in life is critical in the development of a healthy internal representation of the self, the attachment figure, and the external world. A child who has not experienced sensitive care and thus does not believe in the responsiveness of the caregiver is said to have an insecure attachment. This insecure attachment forms a major risk factor in the development of ambivalent relationships, negative mood states, and psychopathology.

For example, Rosenstein and Horowitz examined the relationship among attachment classification, psychopathology, and personality traits in 60 adolescents (13 to 20 years of age) admitted to a psychiatric hospital. An overwhelming majority (97%) of adolescents reported feelings congruent with insecure attachment as described by the Adult Attachment Inventory. Using the diagnostic criteria set forth by the Diagnostic and Statistical Manual of Mental Disorders (3rd ed., revised; DSM-III-R; American Psychiatric Association, 1987), Rosenstein and Horowitz compared the adolescents' psychological assessments. Adolescents labeled as dismissing (i.e., derogatory and cut off from attachment experiences) were associated with conduct and substance abuse disorders as well as denial of psychiatric symptomatology. Those labeled preoccupied (i.e., passive, angry, and entangled by past experiences) were more likely to suffer from affective disorders, and manifested overt disclosure of symptomatic distress.

Thus, the findings were consistent with the internal working models of attachment theory and the vulnerability of early insecure attachments to later psychiatric diagnoses. Researchers concluded that attachment patterns during infancy could serve as an indicator of later psychological problems.

Warren et al. demonstrated a link between attachment classification during infancy and a diagnosis of anxiety disorders during adolescence. Using the Strange Situation as described by Ainsworth et al., Warren et al. classified 164 infants according to patterns of attachment behavior. Of those, 22% (n = 36) were labeled insecure/avoidant and 20% (n = 33) were labeled insecure/resistant. The Schedule for Affective Disorders and Schizophrenia for School-Age Children was then used to determine the presence of anxiety disorders at 17.5 years of age.

The insecure/resistant pattern of attachment was the only classification predictive of future anxiety disorders ($r = .20$, $p < .05$). Twenty-eight percent of the infants labeled as insecure/resistant developed anxiety disorders during adolescence. Those classified as insecure/avoidant were more likely to present other clinical disorders, although the authors did not specify which disorders. These two studies support the significance of attachment measurements as predictors of clinical behavior problems. For a recent review of studies related to infant attachment patterns and later psychopathology, see Dozier, Stovall, and Albus.

REACTIVE ATTACHMENT DISORDER

The Diagnostic and Statistical Manual of Mental Disorders (4th ed.; DSM-IV; American Psychiatric Association, 1994) recognizes Reactive Attachment Disorder (RAD) as one of the most severe forms of infant psychopathology in terms of attachment disturbances. This disorder is characterized by an inability to form normal relationships with others and an impairment in social development, marked by sociopathic behaviors during early childhood.

Richters and Volkmar described numerous cases of children qualifying for a diagnosis of RAD. For example, a young girl diagnosed with RAD developed normally until the age of 3, when she began to display disruptive behaviors. Teachers characterized her as oppositional, impulsive, and alienated from peers due to persistent theft and physical confrontations. Her moods were erratic and fluctuated between clinging and hitting. She reported transient suicidal ideations and usually denied guilt for her disruptive actions.

A more chilling depiction of RAD is given in Reber in his portrayals of various clinical cases. He described a 5-year-old child's smothering of one sibling, his molestation of another, and daily threats of physical violence. In a second example, Reber described how animals are often the recipients of uncontrolled rage. When confronted about setting the dog on fire, one child with RAD replied, "I was just setting my bed on fire and he happened to be under it". These three examples, though varying in the severity of disordered behavior, demonstrate the complexities of the disorder and the extreme pathology exhibited by children with RAD.

Psychologists recognize that the risk for RAD is increased by factors that contribute to abuse and neglect, as in infants who are handicapped or unwanted and/or parent characteristics that interfere with the normative attachment cycle. In terms of caregiver characteristics, such risk factors include parental depression, isolation, and lack of social support, as well as extreme deprivation and abuse during parents' own upbringing. Other risk factors include "difficult" or lethargic infants who may frustrate a caregiver from behaving appropriately, chronically ill infants, lack of contact between caregiver and infant due to hospitalization of either during the first weeks of life, and extended separations from or multiple changes in the primary caregiver.

Although epidemiological data are limited, the DSM-IV describes RAD as a fairly uncommon behavioral disorder marked by developmentally inappropriate social relatedness in most contexts appearing before the age of 5. However, increases in social problems (i.e., family separation, abuse and neglect, and foreign adoptions) may augment the frequency of this disturbance. Reber suggested that this disorder is fairly common, citing a study that claims 1 million children with RAD live in New York city alone. At the time of this writing, the prevalence data for RAD appear to be unclear and inconsistent.

The DSM-IV delineates two subtypes of RAD, the inhibited type and the disinhibited type. The inhibited type is characterized by a persistent failure to initiate and respond to social interactions in a developmentally appropriate manner. There is a resistance to comfort along with a mixed pattern of approach and avoidance behaviors. The disinhibited type is characterized by social promiscuity; the child falls to discriminate attachment behaviors. For example, a child diagnosed with RAD--disinhibited type may be overtly charming, telling strangers that he or she loves them, asking them to come home with him or her. Other features not identified in the current diagnostic criteria of RAD but that appear to be shared by most of these children include lack of empathy, limited eye contact, cruelty to animals, poor impulse control, lack of causal thinking and conscience, abnormal speech patterns, and inappropriate affection with strangers.

These manifestations of RAD occur in early childhood and require immediate clinical intervention. However, indicators of attachment disturbances may be expressed during infancy. A weak crying response and/or tactile defensiveness are causes for alarm. Children at-risk for RAD appear to display either marked stiffness (described as "stiff as a board") or limp posturing. Other indicators include a poor sucking response or little eye contact, as well as no reciprocal smile response and indifference to others. Such signs necessitate clinical assessment and intervention to foster a healthy attachment and counter the emergence of RAD.

Because the behavior associated with RAD often appears similar to (and is often misdiagnosed as) a conduct disorder, oppositional-defiant disorder, or attention deficit hyperactivity disorder, it is important to distinguish those children who show attachment disturbances from those who have other disorders. For this reason, the Randolph Attachment Disorder Questionnaire (RADQ) was developed at the Attachment Center at Evergreen, Colorado as a screening tool for differential diagnoses of children between the ages of 5 and 18 years.

The RADQ is a 30-item, parent-report frequency checklist of various problem behaviors observed throughout the preceding 2 years. It helps to distinguish children with attachment disorders from those with other psychological disturbances as well as to estimate the severity of the attachment disorder. Assessment is best conducted via interview with the child and the parent(s) separately as well as together. In addition, the child's prior history and behavioral responses to systematic separations should be included before a definitive diagnosis of RAD can be made.

Significant changes in the diagnostic criteria for RAD occurred between the revised third edition and the publication of the fourth edition of the DSM. Specifically, the age at onset was raised from 8 months to 5 years (although the diagnosis can be made as early as the first month of life). Original diagnosis included failure of the infant to thrive in terms of growth and development, but this aspect was removed in the fourth edition. Furthermore, the DSM-IV required evidence of pathogenic care in order to diagnose the disorder, thus emphasizing the role of psychosocial factors. Pathogenic care may take the form of persistent disregard of the infant's basic biological and emotional needs or repeated changes in the primary caregiver that prevent the formation of stable attachments.

These criteria have been criticized for many reasons. Specific problems revolve around the focus on social abnormalities rather than maladaptive attachment behaviors, the inclusion of pathogenic parental care in the criteria, the requirement of cross-situational consistency in symptom manifestation, and the representation of maltreatment syndromes rather than attachment disorders. Therefore, the DSM-IV criteria tend to de-emphasize the child's behaviors with the attachment figure, focusing on the reactive" nature of the disorder. Reliance on ill-defined pathogenic etiology as diagnostic criteria may limit the scope of attachment theory applications. Clinicians further the critique by saying that the criteria fail to address the full spectrum of the disorder, allowing diagnosis only in extreme cases of attachment disturbances. This has led to recommendations for diagnostic revision in the case of RAD.

Zeanah pointed out that since the introduction of RAD into the DSM-III, little mention of it has been made throughout the scientific literature, despite an explosion of developmental research on attachment. Zeanah proposed a more complete model of classification, integrating current attachment research to encompass a wider range of attachment disturbances. By incorporating developmental research, the diagnostic criteria can be expanded to include a larger array of children who are in stable, yet dysfunctional attachment relationships.

The system proposed by Zeanah identifies three major types of attachment disturbances: nonattached, disordered, and disrupted. Children classified as nonattached are those over the cognitive age of 10 months who have shown no preferred attachment to anyone. Two subtypes of this group would coincide with the subtypes of the DSM-IV: nonattachment with indiscriminate sociability (disinhibited) and nonattachment with emotional withdrawal (inhibited).

Disordered attachments would characterize those children who do not use the caregiver as a secure base of exploration. Three subtypes of disordered attachment are described: (a) a child who is excessively clingy and inhibited in exploration (disordered attachment with inhibition), (b) a child who fails to check back with the caregiver in times of danger (disordered attachment with self-endangerment), and (c) a child who tends to worry excessively about the emotional well-being of the caregiver (disordered attachment with role-reversal). Disrupted attachment describes the grief response upon the loss of a primary caregiver. Because of the importance of the attachment figure during the first 3 years of life, Zeanah suggested that the loss of the attachment figure at this time would be qualitatively different than at other developmental stages, predisposing a child to problems in attachment.

In the creation of this model of diagnosis, Zeanah reduced the emphasis of past pathogenic history in exchange for observations of the current behavior in the diagnosis of RAD. This focuses more on the attachment--exploration balance and less on abnormal social behavior in the definition of attachment disorders. In doing so, it expands the population to which these criteria could be applied and reduces the clinical confusion involved in ascertaining social functioning. By examining the particular behaviors of the child, this classification is markedly different from the DSM-IV criteria that focus on pervasive disturbances in social relatedness with little attention to the primary attachment characteristics.

Boris, Zeanah, Larrieu, Scheeringa, and Heller used these alternative criteria to conduct the first study of the reliability and validity of diagnostic criteria for attachment disorders in children under 3 years old. To compare the criteria delineated by Zeanah with those from the DSM-IV four independent clinicians assessed 48 clinical case studies from an infant psychiatric clinic.

Greater uniformity in diagnosis in disordered attachment was found using the criteria set forth by Zeanah. Thus, the alternative criteria for attachment disorders appeared to be more reliable diagnostic tools than those of the DSM-IV.

To ascertain the validity of the diagnosis of an attachment disorder, Boris et al. used the Parent--Infant Global Assessment Scale to provide a continuous measure of the adaptive status of the relationship. The mean score on the PGAS for those infants who met the criteria for an attachment disorder was 21 (indicating a "severely disordered" relationship). The mean score for those who did not meet the criteria for an attachment disorder was 47 (indicating a "distressed" relationship). Thus, results of this study showed that those diagnosed with attachment disorders had lower levels of relationship functioning than infants diagnosed with other clinical disorders. Researchers concluded that attachment disorders can be reliably diagnosed without the inclusion of pathogenic care and recommended this criterion be dropped from future diagnostic assessments.

However, RAD is defined as a diagnostic entity, and its presence in childhood may be an indication of future pathological disturbances. Thus, the diagnosis and treatment of RAD are of crucial importance. Numerous therapies have been developed to reach the child with attachment disorders and have met with varying success. These children can be resistant to conventional therapies that are based on a reciprocal relationship of trust because children with RAD do not trust others. Additional barriers to traditional therapies include an inability to profit from experience, a minimal desire to change, little or no regard for authority, and poor impulse control. Regardless of orientation, therapies for those suffering from RAD have similar goals: developing self-control and self-identity, understanding natural consequences, and reinforcing reciprocity and nurturing. These therapies are directed to the individual child, the parent(s), and the family support structure as a whole.

James recommended a residential intervention in which the child lives in an environment conducive to therapeutic parenting. This approach is found at the few attachment centers within the United States. For example, the Attachment Center at Evergreen, Colorado, uses an integrated multidisciplinary approach consisting of therapists, therapeutic foster parents, psychiatric consultants, a clinical director, and a hometown therapist who places parent(s) and child. The 2-week intervention revolves around four key techniques: cognitive re-structuring, re-parenting, psychodramas, and trauma resolution.

A thorough assessment of social history, psychological testing, medical and family assessment, review of prior treatment, and psychiatric evaluation provide the framework for an individualized plan. The child resides with therapeutic foster parents for the duration of the 2 weeks and is allowed minimal interaction with the placing parent(s). The therapeutic parents provide structure and consistency 24 hours a day to the child while working with the placing parent(s) to teach adaptive parenting techniques. Follow-up treatments assess the home life upon release and work to maintain improvements achieved at the facility.

RAD AND HOLDING THERAPY

An additional component of intervention at many such facilities is an unconventional and controversial technique involving physical holding to elicit the child's inner "rage". Holding therapy has been used in this country since its creation in the 1970s. The goal is to recreate the bonding cycle that an infant experiences with the parent. The child lies with his or her head in the lap of the therapist. The child's arms and feet are restrained while the therapist holds the child's head in place to maintain eye contact. The therapist uses confrontational dialogue (e.g., "Who has control?") to invoke inner rage thought to stem from past experiences. This occurs concurrently with positive and nurturing feedback to the child (e.g., "I know you hate, but who ends up suffering?"). Therefore, holding therapy is designed to provide a safe and protected space in which to express overwhelming emotions. Fahlberg cited significant progress in reducing destructive behaviors, strengthening attachments, and increasing emotional expressions following holding therapy.

These holding techniques remain an important component in the treatment of children with RAD at attachment centers across the country. For example, the Attachment Center at Evergreen relies on 30+ hours of holding therapy (3 hours a day for 10 days) during the 2-week intervention described earlier.

Holding therapy is not without its critics. James called holding therapy "cruel, unethical, and potentially dangerous" (p. 94). She likened it to brainwashing, in which individuals are belittled, degraded, and forced into submission. She considered that its benefits would be based on fear rather than on actual attachment formation and called for a halt to the practice, until such time as scientific investigation can support its use.

At this point, empirical support is limited. The few studies to date center on case studies of children admitted for treatment to attachment centers and focus on the intervention in its entirety, not specifically holding therapy. Randolph and Myeroff reported findings of two studies concerning the aforementioned intervention provided at the Attachment Center at Evergreen. One study assessed the behavioral change in 12 children following the intervention compared with a control group of 11 children. Controls were individuals who had expressed interest in treatment but for various reasons were unable to receive it. Both groups completed the Child Behavior Checklist 1 week before and 1 week following the 2-week intensive intervention. Those in the treatment group showed significant decreases in aggression and delinquency as measured by the CBCL, whereas the controls showed no change. Thus, researchers concluded that holding therapy combined with intensive parent counseling was effective in reducing problem behaviors.

The second study assessed 25 children between the ages of 4 and 14 receiving long-term treatment (from 6 months to 2 years) at the same facility. Using the CBCL as a measure of problem behaviors both before and after intervention, Randolph and Myeroff reported significant improvements in behavior for 76% of the sample. About 16% remained unchanged, and 8% showed mixed changes (improved on some subscales and worsened on others). Of those who failed to improve, all but one had multiple psychiatric problems and neurological limitations. Thus, researchers concluded that treatment with these children was more complicated and necessitated additional time to show change. Follow-up evaluations continued to show maintenance of the initial improvements.

Lester presented preliminary findings measuring the amount of behavioral change reported by parents for 12 children (aged 4 to 15 years) admitted to the Attachment and Bonding Center of Ohio. This study evaluated the intervention combining holding therapy, sensory stimulation, and parent counseling. Two scales were used to measure each child's behavioral change. The Devereux Scale of Mental Disorders provides a measure of behaviors related to psychopathology before intervention and at a 4-week follow-up. This is a 110-item scale that derives a total score based on 3 subscores (externalizing behaviors, internalizing behaviors, and critical pathology). The Beech Brook Attachment Disorder Checklist is a 75-item checklist to identify negative and positive attachment behaviors.

Results indicated a significant decrease in the mean Devereux total score, indicating a reduction in psychopathic behaviors. In addition, the mean negative attachment score significantly decreased and the mean positive attachment score increased, indicating an improvement in attachment patterns. Telephone follow-up revealed that all participants were satisfied with their therapy and reported feeling that the intervention was superior to past attempts.

Although these studies have provided favorable support for holding therapy, results should be interpreted cautiously. In each, the effectiveness of the entire residential program was evaluated, not just holding therapy. Small sample sizes, a lack of control groups for two of the three studies, as well as a lack of placebo control prevent results from being attributed to holding therapy over and above other variables.

Additionally, this preliminary evidence provides little validation for the use of such a controversial intervention. Although it may be proposed that holding techniques lower the frequency of aggressive and delinquent behaviors, these studies did not indicate conclusively whether the intervention promotes positive attachment formation. Furthermore, they do not answer the critical question posed by many opponents: Are children who receive this intervention able to form more stable attachments during adolescence or adulthood? Right now, the answer is unclear.

Despite the lack of empirical support, holding therapy continues to attract followers who base their faith on anecdotal evidence. Testimonies of improvements should not be ignored, but they cannot be taken as scientific proof of the efficacy and validity of a practice not yet supported by scientific investigation. Until such time as holding techniques can be empirically validated to improve the condition of RAD without excessive stress to the child, parents may be well advised to consider other options in the treatment of a child with RAD.

CONCLUSIONS

Although research continues on the treatment of RAD, possible causes and subsequent prevention need additional emphasis and study. Identifying common factors in already diagnosed children would help identify populations that may be at risk for developing RAD. One such population may be young children in the foster care system, who face threats far beyond the experiences of normal childhood. Placement in foster care often follows a period of neglect, abuse, exposure to violence, or multiple changes in caregivers either within the natural family or in prior foster care homes. For this reason, Chinitz suggested that the internal working model of the attachment relationship may be disrupted, leaving a child vulnerable to RAD.

The foster care system, by definition, may be problematic. Foster care facilitates interrupted attachment relationships and thus needs to be carefully monitored to ensure stable relationship formation. Foster parents are in a unique situation in that they must learn to deal with a child's displays of hostility, resentment, and ingratitude when they try to offer love. Knowledge of the child's history can help foster parents brace themselves for the rage and distrust that may be prevalent. Foster parents' understanding of the attachment cycle and the subsequent development of disordered attachment is imperative if the foster family is going to stand in good stead to welcome a challenging child into their home.

The attachment cycle is of utmost importance to the healthy social development of our youth. However, science is far behind the clinical observations of the problems that arise when that cycle is disrupted. The challenge is to validate diagnostic criteria for disorders involving the primary relationship from a developmental perspective. Future researchers could use more precise diagnostic instruments to examine the attachment processes and related disorders in high-risk populations. If we are to help our children, we must provide them with the means to develop healthy relationships.

This includes better understanding and appreciation of the attachment cycle as well as further research on the assessment and treatment of those who fail to bond.

2

Childhood Attachment and Adult Attachment in Incarcerated Adult Male Sex Offenders

Stephen W. Smallbone
Mark R. Dadds

Author's Abstract

Forty-eight incarcerated sex offenders were compared with 16 property offenders and 16 nonoffenders on self-report measures of childhood maternal and paternal attachment and adult attachment. The combined sex-offender groups reported significantly less secure maternal, paternal, and adult attachment than did the nonoffenders and significantly less secure maternal attachment than did the property offenders, Intrafamilial child molesters were found to have had particularly problematic relationships with their mothers, reporting a combination of anxious and avoidant qualities in their maternal attachment experiences. By contrast, stranger rapists were found to have had particularly problematic relationships with their fathers and were significantly more likely to have regarded their fathers as having been characteristically unsympathetic, uncaring, abusive, and violent toward them. These results suggest that insecure childhood attachments may be related to offending behavior generally and that certain combinations of childhood attachment experiences may relate more specifically to different kinds of sexual offending.

Childhood Attachment and Adult Attachment in Incarcerated Adult Male Sex Offenders. (Oct 1998), by Mark R Dadds. Journal of Interpersonal Violence, v13 n5, p555(19). Reprinted by permission. References have been removed.

Childhood experiences of male sex offenders have been widely regarded as important by clinicians and researchers seeking to explain the development of sexual offending behavior. Experiences such as disturbed family background; unstable and unnurturing home environments; and frequent, severe, and inconsistent punishment by parents feature among the range of factors observed in the childhood backgrounds of sex offenders.

These childhood experiences, however, may not be unique to the development of sexual offending, and establishing the existence and the nature of these links has been constrained by methodological problems apparent within the existing literature. Relatively few studies, for instance, have systematically compared childhood experiences of sex offenders with other clinical or other offender groups or indeed with nonclinical, nonoffender populations. Those studies that have included control groups have tended to rely on simplistic methods of categorizing sex offenders (e.g., offenders against adults versus offenders against children) that ignore potentially important and possibly systematic differences within such groups. Random sampling of participants, even within special populations such as incarcerated sex offenders, is rarely attempted. Instead, data linking negative childhood experiences with sex offenders have largely been derived from preexisting records of men who either were mandated or volunteered to undergo assessment or treatment and have thus generally been gathered in conditions of limited confidentiality. Under such circumstances, the reliability and validity of data associating sexual offending with negative developmental experiences may be doubtful. The present study aims to address a number of these methodological problems while testing several hypotheses derived from attachment theory concerning the role of childhood experiences in the development of adult sexual offending.

ATTACHMENT BEHAVIOR AND SEXUAL BEHAVIOR

Drawing on evolutionary theory and with extensive reference to ethological data concerning infant-mother interaction, Bowlby described his comprehensive theory of attachment. Earlier ethological research had suggested that infant experiences of maternal interaction may provide a blueprint for subsequent development of other forms of interpersonal behavior (e.g., Harlow & Harlow, 1965). Consistent with this view, Bowlby took a life span perspective of attachment, identifying several fundamental instinctive behavioral systems in humans, notably, the attachment, sexual, and parenting systems, which together serve to promote species survival. He considered that although infant attachment behavior and later sexual behavior are best regarded as separate behavioral systems, there are close linkages between the two. For example, proximity-promoting behaviors in humans such as smiling and clinging are characteristic both of childhood attachment behavior and of adult sexual behavior.

Bowlby originally argued that although infant attachment behavior is biologically programmed, the style of attachment is influenced by environmental factors, particularly those related to the characteristics of the infant attachment figure interaction. For Bowlby, secure attachment arises when needs for proximity and comfort are met by the attachment figure. Under such circumstances, the child is likely to develop confidence in the availability of his caregiver, and this in turn promotes confidence in exploring and interacting with his environment, including other people. Insecure attachment, on the other hand, is likely to arise under conditions in which the caregiver is rejecting, unavailable, or unreliable, and under these conditions, a child is likely to lack confidence in the availability of his caregiver and may consequently interact less confidently with his environment. With the development of cognitive perspective taking, a child's strategies for interacting with his caregiver become organized on the basis of what Bowlby termed a goal-corrected partnership. Within a secure attachment relationship, attempts by the child to influence the behavior of his attachment figure come to be based on a degree of cooperation and mutuality. Within insecure attachment relationships, however, children have been observed to adopt coercive and noncompliant strategies.

Bowlby proposed that the principal evolutionary function of attachment behavior is protection of infants from harm by predators through maintaining proximity to the caregiver. One condition under which the proximity-seeking behavior of infants is most reliably and intensely elicited is that of distress. Harlow revealed an important paradox in the attachment behavior of distressed infants, demonstrating that infant monkeys would cling all the more intensely to rather than avoid a punishing attachment figure. This general observation has been repeated in other animal experiments in which attachment figures have mistreated their infants and appears in part to generalize to human infant attachment behavior. Children of abusive or violent mothers, for example, have been observed to develop disorganized strategies for interacting with their attachment figure, combining aggressive-approach behaviors with ambivalent and avoidant strategies in seemingly unpredictable ways. Although the continuity of early attachment patterns has not yet been demonstrated beyond middle childhood, it may be reasonable to suppose that adults with a history of distressing attachment relationships may be predisposed to respond with intense, disorganized attachment-related behaviors, such as inappropriate sexual behavior, when revisited by distress.

These theoretical links between childhood attachment and adult attachment-related behaviors may have important implications for understanding sexual offending behavior. For securely attached, sexually mature individuals, sexual behavior may tend to be activated within a context that includes perceptions of security, reliability, and mutuality. Other attachment-related behaviors, such as those activated by distress, may be functionally separated from the sexual behavior system, or if they coincide, proximity-seeking behaviors may still be constrained by the set goal of mutuality. For insecurely attached, sexually mature individuals, sexual behavior may be activated with less regard to commitment or mutuality and may indeed be activated in response to negative cognitive and affective states similar to those experienced during problematic early attachment experiences. Disorganization of attachment-related behaviors in adults may result in less functional separation between the attachment and sexual behavior systems, and coercive or contradictory sexual behavior strategies may be employed.

CHILDHOOD ATTACHMENT, ADULT ATTACHMENT, AND SEXUAL OFFENDING

Marshall was the first to introduce concepts of attachment into the discussion of sexual offending, highlighting among sex offenders a characteristic failure to achieve secure childhood and adult attachment bonds. Marshall considered insecure childhood attachment to result in later deficits in interpersonal skills, self-confidence, and empathy, leading to difficulties in engaging in appropriate courtship behaviors and in achieving intimacy in adult relationships. He also suggested that insecurely attached men would tend to meet intimacy needs primarily through sexual activity. Ward, Hudson, Marshall, and Siegert extended Marshall's earlier discussion to consider the role of different insecure adult attachment styles in different forms of sexual offending behavior. Extrapolating from Bartholomew and Horowitz' four-category model of adult attachment, Ward et al. suggested that anxious (preoccupied) adult attachment may predispose some men to sexualize emotional relationships with children and that different forms of avoidant attachment may be associated either with offenses involving no physical contact and/or no emotional investment (fearful attachment) or with aggressive and possibly sadistic sexual offenses (dismissing attachment). A preliminary empirical study provided tentative evidence that sex offenders are insecurely oriented to adult intimate relationships, although insufficient description of offending styles was provided in this study for these researchers to test their more specific hypotheses.

In the present study, we make similar predictions to Ward et al. concerning the relationships between different forms of insecure attachment and different forms of sexual offending, although we make these predictions for somewhat different theoretical reasons. Whereas Ward et al. emphasize the link between adult attachment style and the behavioral strategies employed by sex offenders, we emphasize the link between attachment style and the relationship context within which sexual offending takes place. Consequently, we have defined and identified groups of sex offenders according to the relationship context in which they have been known to offend.

In view of the exploratory nature of our research, two prototypical categories of sexual offenders--men who have had sex with a woman older than the age of 16 years without her expressed or implied consent and with whom they had no prior established relationship (stranger rapists) and men who have had sex with a child younger than the age of 16 years with whom a prior parental relationship existed (intrafamilial child molesters)--were selected for particular attention. Stranger rape is often accompanied by overt hostility, whether the use of actual or threatened violence is instrumental, expressive, or sadistic. In this form of sexual offending, the sexual encounter typically endures no longer than is required for sexual gratification and by definition, the sexual act occurs outside any established relationship. In contrast, the offending of intrafamilial child molesters typically involves a pseudo courtship sequence, often referred to as grooming, and by definition, occurs within the context of a preexisting parent-child relationship. Intrafamilial child molesters often describe their offending as being motivated by a felt need for affection or intimacy. Thus, intrafamilial child molestation is often less overtly agressive, and the relationship surrounding the sexual interaction is more enduring than it is in stranger rape.

These differences in relationship contexts suggest that the quality of attachment in stranger rapists and intrafamilial child molesters may be quite different, although both may share certain aspects of disorganization of attachment-related behaviors. The offending of stranger rapists appears consistent with a largely avoidant attachment style, an implication supported by the general lack of commitment by rapists to adult intimate relationships. This implication is further supported by observations of avoidant children, who have been observed to be more hostile and less empathic than other children and who may threaten or attack their attachment figure. By contrast, the offending of intrafamilial child molesters appears consistent with a more anxious attachment style. Recourse to sexual contact with intrafamilial children is known often to occur in a context of instability in the adult relationship. The approval-seeking features of anxious attachment, together with a tendency to sexualize love relationships, may help to explain the response by intrafamilial offenders to perceived unavailability of their marital partners by seeking sexual contact with a less threatening and more available female.

A third category of sex offenders--men who have had sex with a child younger than the age of 16 years outside a family context (extrafamilial child molesters)--has also been included in this study. The expected relationship between attachment and sexual behavior in these men is somewhat less clear, however, and no specific predictions are made for this group in the current study other than that they will be characterized generally by an insecure attachment style. Extrafamilial offenders may share certain contextual/behavioral features with rapists and intrafamilial offenders and are included in this study for exploratory rather than for strong theoretical reasons.

To test these speculations, improvements in research design need to be made to determine the specificity of attachment problems to sexual offending. In this study, several methodological improvements are attempted. These include (a) examination of the reliability of reports of attachment experiences in an incarcerated sex-offender population, (b) use of a more random sample of sex offenders than those participating in assessment or treatment, (c) provision of confidentiality of the information provided by offenders, (d) application of more stringent criteria for inclusion of participants in offender groups, and (e) use of both nonoffender and non-sex offender comparison groups.

Two general hypotheses and two specific hypotheses concerning sex offenders were tested in this study. First, it was predicted that sex offenders would be characterized overall by less secure childhood and adult attachment than would nonoffenders. Second, it was predicted that sex offenders would report less secure childhood and adult attachment than would non-sex offenders. Third, intrafamilial child molesters were expected to be characterized by more anxious attachment than were all other groups. Fourth, stranger rapists were expected to be characterized by more avoidant attachment than were all other groups.

METHOD

Participants

Sixteen convicted and incarcerated adult rapists whose victims were unknown to them, 16 intrafamilial child molesters, and 16 extrafamilial child molesters were recruited from three correctional centers in South East Queensland, Australia. A comparison group comprising 16 incarcerated property offenders was also recruited from one of these correctional centers. The property offenders had no documented history of sexual offenses or offenses of violence against persons and served to control for the possible confounding effects of general criminality and incarceration. Sixteen male custodial correctional officers were recruited from one of these correctional centers as a nonoffending comparison group. By virtue of the screening processes undertaken for their employment, correctional officers were known to have no recorded criminal history.

Offenders were initially randomly identified through prison nominal rolls that list offenders according to their most serious current offenses. Prison files were then examined, and demographic and offense-history data were gathered on prospective participants. Offenders were excluded from the study if their offending history identified offenses belonging to more than one offense category. The groups differed significantly in age, $F(4, 74) = 15.96$, p [is less than] .001, with Tukey's HSD test revealing that the nonoffenders ($M = 40.3$, $SD = 6.5$), the intrafamilial child molesters ($M = 40.9$, $SD = 7.4$), and the extrafamilial child molesters ($M = 44.5$, $SD = 9.5$) were significantly older than were the property offenders ($M = 26.9$, $SD = 7.0$) and rapists ($M = 29.5$, $SD = 7.7$). The groups did not differ in socioeconomic status.

Offense history data revealed that of the three sex offender groups, the extrafamilial child molesters were the most likely to have had prior convictions for sexual offending (81%), and the stranger rapists were the most likely to have had prior convictions for nonsexual violent offending (50%). All the property offenders had prior convictions for property offending.

Self-Report Measures

A variety of retrospective measures of childhood attachment exist, ranging from the relatively complex semistructured Adult Attachment Interview to simple self-report instruments (e.g., Hazan & Shaver, 1986, in Collins & Read, 1990). Given the specialized population of the present study, we were interested in using measures that provided (a) low levels of intrusiveness, (b) high levels of confidentiality, and (c) ease of administration. For theoretical reasons, we were further interested in choosing measures of childhood and adult attachment that measured the same childhood and adult attachment styles. Consequently, the following self-report measures were selected.

A childhood attachment questionnaire was used as a retrospective measure of childhood attachment. This questionnaire contains three descriptions characterizing caregiving styles consistent with Ainsworth, Blehar, Waters, and Wall's original three childhood attachment styles (secure; anxious/ambivalent; avoidant). The three descriptions appeared twice in the questionnaire booklet used in this study: first in relation to the respondent's relationship with his mother, then with his father. Ratings were made on Likert-type scales ranging from 1 (not at all like my mother) to 7 (very much like my mother).

The Relationship Scales Questionnaire (RSQ) contains 30 short statements (e.g. "It is very important for me to feel independent; .... My desire to get close often scares people away") that participants rated on a scale of 1 (not at all like me) to 5 (very much like me). The RSQ provides measures of adult attachment style and can be scored to obtain measures of the same three attachment styles as can the childhood attachment measure (secure; anxious; avoidant), thus allowing for correlational analysis to assess theoretically expected continuity between childhood and adult attachment styles.

An attachment history checklist, similar to that used by Hazan and Shaver, was used as a retrospective measure of the quality of family relationships during childhood. In comparison to the childhood attachment questionnaire described above, the attachment history checklist allows for more specific patterns of childhood attachment relationships to be identified. As we expected that sex offenders would have experienced relatively severe attachment problems that might otherwise not be identified with available standard measures, the two adjectives "abusive" and "violent" were added to this checklist. Participants were simply asked to tick any of 19 adjectives (e.g., responsive, rejecting, inconsistent, violent) that described the attitudes, feelings, and behaviors of their mothers toward them and of their fathers toward them.

Procedure

All offenders were approached individually by the first author, a prison-based psychologist, and asked to participate in a study of childhood and adult relationships. Offenders were assured that they would incur no penalty if they declined to participate and that their responses would be treated with the strictest confidence. A point was made of explaining that the information provided would not be used within the prison system and that completed questionnaires would not be stored on-site. They were told that a number would be assigned to their questionnaires and that once additional information was obtained from their prison files, any record of their names would be destroyed. Correctional officers were told that they were serving as a nonoffending comparison group for the purposes of a study examining childhood and adult relationships among sex offenders and were provided complete anonymity. Response rates for the groups were as follows: correctional officers, 59.25%; property offenders, 94.12%; rapists, 55.00%; intrafamilial child molesters, 76.19%; and extrafamilial child molesters, 100.00%.

RESULTS

Test-Retest Reliability

Prior to conducting the main study, 18 sex offenders participating in a custodial-based treatment program were recruited for a preliminary study that aimed to determine the test-retest reliability of the set of questionnaires, described above, among an incarcerated sex-offender population. Prospective participants were asked by the first author if they would participate in a study aimed at assessing the usefulness of a set of questionnaires. They were told that this study bore no direct relation to their treatment program and that participation would be anonymous and voluntary. All men approached agreed to participate. Each participant completed the questionnaire booklet twice during an interval of 3 weeks.

With the exception of paternal anxious attachment ratings, all childhood attachment ratings were moderately to strongly stable, with Pearson correlation coefficients ranging from .51 (paternal avoidant attachment) to .93 (paternal secure attachment). Adult attachment too was generally stable, with Pearson correlation coefficients ranging from .46 (secure) to .89 (anxious). Items from the attachment history checklist were also generally stable. Kappa coefficients for the 19 adjectives describing maternal attachment relationships ranged from .45 (mother intrusive, mother inconsistent) to 1.00 (mother understanding, mother violent) (M = .75, SD =. 17); those describing paternal attachment relationships ranged from .31 (father intrusive) to 1.00 (father abusive, father strict, father overprotective) (M = .69, SD = .25). Thus, with the exception of a few items, our self-report measures were found generally to be stable among a sample of incarcerated sex offenders. Test-retest data were not included in the main study, to which we now return.

CORRELATIONS BETWEEN CHILDHOOD AND ADULT ATTACHMENT

Despite the theoretically expected continuity between childhood and adult attachment styles, these were at best moderately correlated. Secure childhood attachment to mother was moderately correlated with the RSQ measure of secure adult attachment, $r = .35$, p [is less than] .01. Anxious attachment to mother, $r = .35$, p [is less than] .01, and avoidant attachment to mother, $r = .28$, p [is less than] .01, were moderately correlated with anxious and avoidant adult attachment, respectively. None of the three paternal attachment styles predicted their respective adult attachment styles.

Differences Between Sex Offenders and Nonoffenders
The hypothesis that sex offenders would be characterized by less secure (maternal and paternal) childhood and adult attachment than would nonoffenders was tested by conducting three one-way ANOVAs. As each of the three analyses was testing directional hypotheses, one-tailed p values were used to evaluate significance. Scores for the three sex-offender groups were combined and compared with those of the correctional officers. Table 1 presents the mean ratings of maternal and paternal childhood attachment and of adult attachment for the correctional officers and the combined sex-offenders group.

TABLE 1: Mean Ratings (SDs) of Childhood and Adult Attachment

		Maternal(a)		
Group	n	Secure	Anxious	Avoidant
Correctional officers	16	6.4	1.7	1.2
		(1.3)	(1.0)	(0.8)
Property offenders	16	4.4	4.1	2.7
		(2.4)	(2.0)	(2.3)
Combined sex offenders	48	3.5	3.4	3.3
		(2.4)	(2.0)	(2.5)
Stranger rapists	16	2.9	3.6	3.3
		(2.0)	(1.9)	(2.5)
Intrafamilial child molesters	16	3.5	3.1	3.9
		(2.5)	(2.3)	(2.6)
Extrafamilial child molesters	16	4.1	3.3	2.9
		(2.4)	(1.9)	(2.7)

Paternal(a)

Group	Secure	Anxious	Avoidant
Correctional officers	5.0	3.5	2.0
	(1.9)	(2.3)	(2.0)
Property offenders	2.9	3.9	4.3
	(2.0)	(1.8)	(2.6)
Combined sex offenders	3.0	3.5	3.6
	(2.1)	(2.0)	(2.4)
Stranger rapists	2.4	3.4	4.3
	(1.5)	(2.0)	(2.5)
Intrafamilial child molesters	3.3	3.6	3.3
	(2.6)	(2.5)	(2.5)
Extrafamilial child molesters	3.1	3.4	3.4
	(2.1)	(1.0)	(2.4)

Adult(b)

Group	Secure	Anxious	Avoidant
Correctional officers	3.7	2.1	2.1
	(0.7)	(1.1)	(0.9)
Property offenders	3.1	2.8	3.2
	(0.6)	(1.1)	(0.8)
Combined sex offenders	3.0	2.9	3.3
	(0.9)	(1.0)	(1.0)
Stranger rapists	2.9	3.1	3.6
	(0.8)	(1.1)	(0.9)
Intrafamilial child molesters	3.0	3.1	3.3
	(1.0)	(1.0)	(1.1)
Extrafamilial child molesters	3.1	2.6	3.2
	(0.8)	(1.0)	(0.9)

(a.) Ratings provided on a scale of 1 to 7.

(b.) Ratings provided on a scale of 1 to 5.

As predicted, the sex offenders were found to be significantly less secure in their maternal childhood attachment than were the nonoffenders, $F(1, 62) = 22.14$, p [is less than] .0001. Sex offenders were also found to report less secure attachment to their fathers than were the nonoffenders, $F(1, 58) = 11.77$, p [is less than] .001. Adult attachment too was significantly different between these groups, with sex offenders less secure in their orientation to adult intimate relationships than were nonoffenders, $F(1, 61) = 6.49$, p = .001.

DIFFERENCES BETWEEN SEX OFFENDERS AND NON SEX OFFENDERS

The hypothesis that sex offenders as a combined group would report less secure childhood and adult attachment than would non-sex (i.e., property) offenders was tested by three separate ANCOVAs, using age as a covariate (preliminary analysis had revealed that the combined sex-offender groups were significantly older than were the non-sex offenders). Once again, one-tailed p values were used to evaluate significance. As predicted, the sex offenders were significantly less secure in their childhood maternal attachments than were the property offenders, $F(1, 61) = 3.08$, p = .042. The sex offenders, however, were less secure in neither their childhood paternal attachment nor in their adult attachment than were the property offenders.

ANXIOUS ATTACHMENT AND INTRAFAMILIAL CHILD MOLESTERS

The hypothesis that intrafamilial child molesters would report higher levels of anxious attachment than all other groups was tested in two ways. First, three separate ANCOVAs, again using age as a covariate, were performed to analyze data on the continuous, global measures of maternal anxious, paternal anxious, and adult anxious attachment. Second, differences in the quality of childhood maternal and paternal relationships using the attachment history checklist were examined by a series of chi-square analyses (see Table 2). The reader should note that Bonferroni correction for these multiple chi-square analyses would result in alpha levels of p = .002. Due to the exploratory nature of the present research and the possible measurement error suggested by the moderate stability of some of our measures, uncorrected probability values were used to evaluate significance.

TABLE 2: Participants in Each Group Who Endorsed Significant
Attachment History Descriptors (in percentages)

	Group		
Descriptor	Correctional Officers (n = 16)	Property Offenders (n = 16)	Stranger Rapists (n = 16)
Mother			
Loving	94	88	69
Accepting	81	69	31
Attentive	75	31	19
Sympathetic	88	50	38
Understanding	94	69	50
Inconsistent	13	44	38
Unresponsive	13	25	31
Rejecting	6	19	38
Abusive	13	13	19
Father			
Caring	69	29	13
Sympathetic	50	36	0
Respectful	69	21	13
Understanding	69	29	13
Abusive	13	36	67
Violent	13	29	67

122

Descriptor	Intrafamilial Child Molesters (n = 16)	Extramilial Child Molesters (n16)	Chi-Square
Mother			
Loving	38	63	p = .004
Accepting	44	44	p = .029
Attentive	31	31	p = .012
Sympathetic	31	25	p = .003
Understanding	31	44	p = .003
Inconsistent	69	25	p = .015
Unresponsive	63	38	p = .043
Rejecting	56	25	p = .023
Abusive	56	19	p = .017
Father			
Caring	50	57	p = .031
Sympathetic	31	29	p = .043
Respectful	44	50	p = .013
Understanding	38	50	p = .023
Abusive	44	36	p = .043
Violent	31	21	p = .047

The results of the three ANCOVAs did not support our hypothesis. No significant differences between groups were found on the continuous measures of maternal anxious, paternal anxious, and adult anxious attachment. The results of the chi-square analyses, however, revealed a distinctive pattern of relationship variables among the intrafamilial child molesters. Specifically, these offenders were significantly more likely than any other group to have regarded their mothers as having been unloving, $X:(4) = 15.12, p = .004$; unresponsive, $X:(4) = 9.84$, $p = .043$; inconsistent, $X2(4) = 12.27$, $p = .015$; rejecting, $X2(4) = 11.35, p = .023$; and abusive, $X2(4) = 12.01, p = .017$, toward them.

AVOIDANT ATTACHMENT AND STRANGER RAPISTS

The hypothesis that stranger rapists would report more avoidant attachment than would other groups was also not supported by the results of three separate ANCOVAs, again controlling for age and using data from the three global avoidant attachment measures. Maternal avoidant, $F(4, 73) = 3.02$, $p = .023$, and adult avoidant attachment, $F(4, 73) = 5.17$, $p = .001$, were significantly different overall but despite a nonsignificant trend for rapists to report higher levels of avoidant adult attachment, the rapists were not significantly more avoidant than was any other group. However, the chi-square analyses revealed a pattern of avoidant-type parental relationship variables among the rapists. Together with the other sex offenders, the rapists were more likely to regard their mothers as not understanding, not sympathetic, and not accepting. Specifically, however, the rapists were significantly more likely than was any other group to report their fathers as having been not caring, [chi square](4) = 10.60, p = .031; not sympathetic, [chi square](4) = 9.83, p = .043; abusive, [chi square](4) = 9.86, p = .043; and violent, [chi square](4) = 11.88, p = .018, toward them.

DISCUSSION

This study examined childhood attachment and adult attachment in three different adult sex-offender groups (i.e., stranger rapists, intrafamilial child molesters, and extrafamilial child molesters), a non-sex offender group (i.e., property offenders), and a nonoffender group (i.e., correctional officers). Two general and two specific hypotheses concerning the relationship between attachment experiences and sexual offending were tested.

The hypothesis that sex offenders would report less secure childhood and adult attachment than would nonoffenders was supported by the results of this study. Ratings of childhood maternal, childhood paternal, and adult secure attachment were all found to discriminate sex offenders from honor fenders. These findings support Marshall's and Ward et al.'s speculations that sex offenders are likely to have experienced insecure childhood attachments and that they would be insecurely oriented to adult intimate relationships. These results also support the findings of Ward et al., and extend these previous findings in two important ways. First, our results provide the first empirical evidence that sex offenders have experienced insecure childhood attachments. Second, our results provide evidence that these insecure attachments may be linked to childhood relationships with both mother and father.

The second hypothesis narrowed the focus of our exploration somewhat. Here, we predicted that incarcerated sex offenders would report less secure childhood and adult attachment than would similarly incarcerated offenders who had no documented history of violent or sexual offending (i.e., property offenders). Our results provided partial support for this hypothesis. After controlling for age differences, the sex offenders were less secure in their childhood maternal attachment than were the property offenders. The sex offenders were not, however, found to be less secure than were the property offenders in relation to their fathers and were not less securely oriented to adult intimate relationships than were other offenders. These findings suggest that insecure attachments may relate generally to offending behavior and that the relationship of these insecure attachments to sexual offending either may be nonspecific or may be more specific than our general measures could reveal. Differences between the sex offenders and the property offenders in the quality of childhood maternal attachment were, however, also found on the attachment history checklist. Sex offenders as a group were more likely than were the nonoffenders and tended to be more likely than were the property offenders to have regarded their mothers as not understanding and not sympathetic toward them and as having been not accepting of them. Together, these results provide at least tentative evidence for the specificity of insecure maternal attachment with regard to sexual offending, over and above its possibly more general influence on criminality.

Our third and fourth hypotheses were yet more specific. Here, we explored attachment-related differences between different categories of sex offenders and, in particular, predicted anxious attachment patterns among the intrafamilial child molesters and avoidant patterns among the stranger rapists. Although no differences emerged in relation to the more global measures of anxious or avoidant adult attachment, distinctive patterns of maternal and paternal attachment history were found. Although these were largely consistent with our predictions, the differences between the intrafamilial child molesters and stranger rapists with regard to their maternal and paternal attachment histories are particularly noteworthy. The intrafamilial child molesters had experienced particularly problematic relationships with their mothers. These childhood maternal relationships involved both anxious (mother inconsistent and unresponsive) and avoidant (mother rejecting and abusive) patterns. In contrast, the stranger rapists experienced particularly problematic, more clearly avoidant relationships with their fathers, whom they regarded as having been uncaring, unsympathetic, abusive, and violent toward them.

The rapists in this study resembled the property offenders in several important respects. Both the rapists and the property offenders reported relatively problematic attachment relationships with their fathers. Both groups had come to prison early, relative to the other offender groups, and the great majority of the rapists studied had previously been convicted of having committed property offenses. The distinguishing feature of the rapists in this study, however, was the remarkable frequency with which they reported characteristically abusive and violent childhood relationships with their fathers. These early experiences of paternal abuse and violence, hallmarks of disorganized childhood attachment behavior, may add critically to rapists' already exceptionally low levels of secure maternal attachment by confirming their expectations that they are unworthy of close relationships. If they indeed seek out adult intimate relationships, they may adopt an uncaring, unsympathetic approach to their partners. Their sexual behavior may become disconnected from normal (i.e., secure) attachment-related perceptions, such as commitment and mutuality, and may be readily activated or at least may fail to be inhibited in the context of abuse and violence.

More than half of the intrafamilial child molesters reported that their mothers had been characteristically abusive toward them. Intrafamilial child molesters may thus be predisposed to engage sexually, not necessarily in the context of violence, but perhaps without due regard to mutuality. These offenders may bring with them to their adult intimate relationships expectations that their partner will be unloving, unresponsive, inconsistent, and rejecting. Moreover, the sexual behavior of these men may not be disinhibited and indeed may be especially activated within the context of interpersonal abuse.

Although no specific predictions were made concerning the extrafamilial child molesters, it is nevertheless noteworthy that no distinguishing feature of this group emerged in the results of this study. This is somewhat surprising given that this group was the most chronic in terms of sexual offending (81% had been previously convicted of sexual offenses against children) and that many might be regarded as having an exclusive sexual orientation toward children. Such offenders are often regarded as the most disturbed in terms of their sexual behavior. Given that a number of these offenders may have had no intimate or sexual experiences with other adults, their responses to the adult attachment measures may have in fact reflected their intimate experiences with children and so may be particularly inaccurate with regard to the purposes of the current study. This does not, however, explain their unremarkable responses to the childhood attachment measures. Main has suggested that particularly troubled adults tend to reflect incoherently on early attachment experiences, overestimating the degree of secure attachment. It is possible that the simple self-report measures used in the present study may have obscured levels of insecure childhood attachment that might otherwise have been identified, say, on the basis of the Adult Attachment Interview.

The reliable and valid measurement of childhood and adult attachment in sex offenders may continue to present problems to researchers seeking to establish the specificity of attachment-related problems among this population. Although the measures used in the present study were shown generally to have at least moderate stability and served our purposes of unintrusiveness, confidentiality, ease of administration, and internal consistency, self-report methods generally are unlikely to circumvent the high levels of defensiveness or distortion known to be particularly common both among sexual offenders and among nonoffending adults when reflecting on insecure childhood attachments. Thus, the findings of the present study may underestimate the presence and the degree of childhood attachment problems generally among sex offenders.

Apart from these measurement problems, several other limitations of the present study deserve mention. First, our power analysis was conducted on the assumption of moderate to large effect sizes. Larger group numbers may have revealed differences of smaller effect sizes, especially those expected between different subgroups of sex offenders. Second, our examination of childhood attachments is vulnerable to the usual limitations of retrospective studies. In particular, results of the childhood attachment measures may represent current constructions of past events rather than actual biography and so may have limited construct validity. Moreover, it is unclear whether the differences between groups indicate causality or whether these differences may only exist retrospectively. Finally, despite our attempts to use random-sampling methods, almost half of the stranger rapists approached to participate in this study declined to do so. Some who declined commented that their relationships with their parents were so distressing that they did not wish to be reminded of it. Our sample of stranger rapists may thus seriously under-represent the extent of attachment problems among this group.

Despite its limitations, however, the present study has provided at least tentative empirical evidence of problematic childhood experiences among incarcerated sex offenders while controlling for criminality and incarceration. Other carefully designed studies are required to further identify the commonalities and differences in attachment experiences between offenders and nonoffenders, between sex offenders and other offenders, and between various subtypes of sex offenders. The fundamental theoretical link between attachment and sexuality offers researchers of sexual offending a sound, albeit largely unexplored, theoretical base from which these problem behaviors might more rigorously be investigated.

In conclusion, the results of the present study suggest that early insecure attachment experiences may place some men at risk of later offending. More particularly, they suggest that certain combinations of attachment-related experiences may place some men at risk to offend sexually within a particular interpersonal context. Although much work is needed to identify the more specific effects of early attachment-related problems to later sexual behavior problems, the present study represents a tentative but important step in incorporating attachment theory into the study of sexual offending and in recognizing that sexual offending may usefully be understood in terms of the relationship context within which it takes place. We believe that further research into the link between attachment and both normal and deviant sexual behavior is warranted.

Stephen W. Smallbone is currently a lecturer in the School of Justice Administration and an adjunct lecturer in clinical psychology in the School of Applied Psychology at Griffith University in Queensland, Australia. He has extensive experience in the assessment and treatment of sex offenders and in program development, in both custodial and community settings. The current research was conducted as part of his doctoral program at Griffith University.

Mark R. Dadds is currently a professor of psychology and director of research in the School of Applied Psychology at Griffith University in Queensland, Australia. He has extensive experience in clinical, research, and organizational aspects of child and family psychology. He directs several national intervention programs for children, youth, and their families who are at risk for mental health problems and works on a number of programs for children and families who have experienced violence, abuse, and breakdown. He has authored more than 70 articles and two books on child and family psychology.

3

Mother/Child Bonding: Incarcerated Women Struggle to Maintain Meaningful Relationships with their Children

Joann B. Morton
Deborah M. Williams

Abstract

Correctional administrators have developed programs that help incarcerated mothers build and maintain meaningful and positive relationships with their children, in recognition of the importance of the mother/child bond in a child's development. Many creative programs have been developed, such as a formal prison nursery for young children of women inmates, the Mothers and Their Children program and the Girl Scouts Beyond Bars program. However, prison administrators face several challenges in instituting such programs, foremost among which is a prison environment that discourages visits from children.

The importance of bonding among men has become a topic of public debate in the last few years as various religious and ethnic groups have encouraged men to meet and form common ties. Since almost 40 percent of children in the United States do not live with their biological fathers, increased attention also has been given to the importance of the bond between fathers and their children.

Mother-child bonding: Incarcerated women's struggle to maintain meaningful relationships with their children, by Joanne B. Morton and Deborah M. Williams. Corrections Today, Dec 1998 v60 i7 p. 98(6). Reprinted by permission. References and endnotes have been removed.

Often overlooked in this debate is the powerful role that mothers play in the development of the physical and emotional health of their children. From birth, mothers often are the ones who encourage the first smiles, words and steps from their babies. Mothers traditionally are the ones who provide the unconditional love that babies need to develop strong relationships with others in the future.

For incarcerated women, developing and maintaining meaningful relationships with their children is difficult. The most common concerns voiced by mothers in prison revolve around what is happening to their children while they are gone. More than 56,000 children have mothers in prison. These children miss their mothers and have difficulty understanding why they cannot be with them.

But bonding is a two-way street. The opportunity to develop meaningful relationships is important to the emotional health and feelings of self-worth of both incarcerated mothers and their children. Recognizing the importance of bonding, correctional administrators over time have developed programs to help maintain and strengthen relationships between incarcerated women and their children.

INCARCERATED MOTHERS

The growth in the number of women offenders in all parts of the criminal justice system has been well-documented. The number of women incarcerated at state and federal levels is approaching 80,000, while the number of women in the nation's jails is reaching 10 percent of the total, short-term facility population.

Add to this the following facts and the need for women offenders to maintain and strengthen ties with their children becomes more obvious.

* 25 percent of women admitted to prison are pregnant or have recently delivered a child;

* 74 percent of women in prison have children, compared to 64 percent of men;

* Incarceration of a mother disrupts the family considerably more than incarceration of a father;

* 25 percent of incarcerated women's children live with their fathers, compared to 90 percent of incarcerated men's children who live with the children's mothers;

* 65 percent of incarcerated women's children live with grandparents and 10 percent are in foster care;

* 90 percent of incarcerated women have contact with their children while in prison, compared to 80 percent of incarcerated men;

* More than 50 percent of incarcerated women with children under 18 never have visits from their children; and

* The majority of women believe they will have responsibility for their children upon release.

MOTHER/CHILD RELATIONSHIPS

Studies have shown that the effects of maternal deprivation are widespread. Young children who are removed from their mothers for hospitalization or other reasons display immediate distress, followed by misery and apathy. Another, much more serious effect of maternal deprivation is developmental retardation and general impairment of developmental progress. The longer the period of separation between the child and its mother, the greater the disturbance.

However, the idea that there is some mystical relationship between a mother and a young child has been rejected in recent years. Rather than a golden period in which mother/child relationships must be fostered, researchers stress the importance of the quality of the relationship between the child and his or her mother or other significant caregivers at different stages in the child's life.

The quality of the mother/child relationship sets the stage for all other relationships that the child will have. Positive interaction in the child's early years is critical to the development of healthy social relationships and personality growth. Young children internalize values and social norms based upon positive interactions with their parents.

The bond between mother and child becomes even more important as the child reaches adolescence A great deal of a teenager's time is spent in testing the ideologies and roles of adult life. While the prospect of becoming an adult is exciting to a teenager, it also is very confusing and frightening. A strong bond with a parent provides a safe and healthy outlet for teen-age expression. Children separated from their mothers and fathers at this crucial juncture have a very difficult time establishing a healthy sense of their own identities.

The interactions between a child and its parents form mutually shared expectations and norms. The shared intimacy, conversation and humor involved in normal parent-child interactions establish the framework for the child to be able to maintain intimate relationships of his or her own when the child reaches adolescence and adulthood.

Since the children of incarcerated women often do not have fathers present in their lives, the mother's role in their ongoing social and emotional developments can be important. The absence of this bond may account for many of the problems that children of incarcerated women have in school and the high correlation between incarcerated mothers and delinquency among their children.

CORRECTIONS AND MOTHERHOOD

One of the most serious pains of imprisonment for a mother is to be separated from her children. Even if her relationships with her children were less than ideal when she was in the community, she may develop unrealistic memories of that time. She may want to be the "perfect mother" but may not have the skills to meet the emotional and physical needs of her children upon release. It does not help if the children become hostile toward her and blame her for their discomfort while she is gone. Indeed, children frequently resent and fail to obey mothers who have been incarcerated. Mothers, in turn, feel guilty about their period of separation, and may overcompensate when trying to discipline or instruct their children.

Correctional administrators do not make the decision to incarcerate mothers, nor do they determine when they can be released. Many, particularly those working in women's institutions, are sensitive to the need for meaningful and positive contact between mothers and their children. They courageously support the development and maintenance of programs in spite of political and public outcries to make prison so miserable that people will be deterred from committing further crimes.

But prison administrators face a number of challenges when developing programs to maintain ties between incarcerated mothers and their children. In many instances, the prison environment discourages visits from children and their guardians. Long distances to facilities, lack of public transportation, invasive search procedures, crowding and limitations in having food in visiting areas are among the problems that must be overcome in establishing programs for women and their children. In some short-term facilities, young children are not allowed to visit, and in others, no physical contact is permitted between children and their mothers. Agency visiting policies designed for male facilities may place limits on what can be done in women's institutions, particularly when wardens are not allowed to modify policies and practices to meet the needs of incarcerated women. Fear of liability and the regulations of other agencies and organizations also may pose problems.

In spite of the many barriers to be overcome, a number of creative programs have evolved over time. One of the first to be implemented was a formal prison nursery to house the young children of women inmates.

IN THE BEGINNING

It was common practice in both England and the American Colonies to incarcerate babies and young children with their mothers. However, the conditions were horrendous and many of the children and their mothers died. The late 1800s witnessed an emphasis on improving conditions for women in prison, and since reinforcing women's traditional roles as wives and mothers was considered essential to their reformation, early programs focused on bonding between women and their young children. In the New York Reformatory for Women at Bedford Hills, under the progressive leadership of Dr. Katherine B. Davis, a nursery for inmates' children was established in 1901. Other states followed suit and in the 1920s and 1930s, prison nurseries were fairly common in women's institutions around the country. By the late 1960s and early 1970s, the popularity of nurseries began to wan and some states passed laws prohibiting children from living in prison.

Today, only two states - Nebraska and New York - operate nurseries for children. Both programs stress the development of nurturing behavior by the mother and provide parenting classes for women to learn and practice positive child-rearing skills. The Nebraska program also includes overnight visits for older children.

Other facilities have camps for children and their mothers to encourage bonding. The Pocatello Women's Correctional Center in Idaho sponsored a camp last summer for women who had gone through the facility's parenting program. The camp was an excellent example of cooperation and collaboration between the facility and a variety of other agencies and groups, including the local hospital, churches and the university.

Given that a large number of women offenders can be classified as minimum security, many advocate that women be allowed to remain in the community following their convictions or be transferred from prison to a community residential setting to deliver their babies and keep them in that environment. The Federal Bureau of Prisons operates the Mothers and Infants in Transition (MINT) program, in which selected pregnant minimum security women can be moved to community programs prior to delivery and remain there for a specified period of time following birth. This program enables a woman to be in a supportive environment during the latter stages of her pregnancy and bond with her child following its birth. Some 17 states make available community facilities that can accommodate children as an alternative to prison for women who have committed minor crimes or as transition centers for those leaving prison. These programs are less intrusive on the mother/child relationship than is prison; are more cost-effective than institutionalization; provide for supportive development and practice of child-care skills; and can accommodate children older than two.

Other programs target nonresidential activities for both younger and older children. An important part of the Nebraska mother/child program is the Mother Offspring Life Development (MOLD) component, designed in 1976 to foster positive relationships between incarcerated mothers and their children when the children are at home. The Mothers and Their Children (MATCH) program was started by the National Council on Crime and Delinquency in 1978, and has been replicated in 11 states. It focuses on improving visiting procedures, developing children's centers where women and children can play and learn together, and implementing a variety of supportive and educational services.

The Pennsylvania Department of Corrections' State Correctional Institution at Muncy has developed an innovative program called I Love You This Much. It consists of a workbook, developed by staff and inmates, designed to help mothers communicate effectively with their children, and provides examples of ways that incarcerated mothers can "take an active role in the child's development, guidance and daily life" through letters and activities.

Perhaps one of the most innovative and successful programs established to encourage interaction between mothers and their children is the Girl Scouts Beyond Bars program. The pilot for this program was implemented in 1992 by the National Institute of Justice in cooperation with the Girl Scouts of America and the Maryland Correctional Institution for Women. With the support of the local Girl Scout Council, a Girl Scout troop was formed for the daughters of female inmates. The girls have regular scout meetings in the community, where they participate in normal Girl Scout activities. Then, twice a month, the scout meetings are held at the women's facility. During these meetings, the mothers and their daughters participate in a variety of activities and troop projects, such as puppet shows and structured play, as well as more serious discussions of self-esteem, drug abuse, relationships, pregnancy prevention and coping with family crisis. After its initial success in Maryland, the program has been replicated in a number of jurisdictions across the country.

Conclusion

Wide variation exists in the quantity and quality of programs and services in women's institutions geared toward maintaining and strengthening ties between mothers and their children. Disturbing trends were revealed in a 1995 survey of the 50 states, the District of Columbia and three Canadian provinces, which found that fewer women's institutions offered parenting classes, furloughs, overnight visits with children and children's centers in 1996 than in 1985. On a positive note, considerably more facilities provided access to community facilities for mothers and children. But even here, only 23 women's facilities out of 86 institutions had such programs.

As Life magazine writer Claudia Dowling so eloquently states, "A mother may be guilty, but a child is always innocent." With the dramatic increase in the number of incarcerated women in America's prisons, we cannot afford to expand the "get tough" philosophy to offenders' children. This issue needs the active involvement of correctional administrators and staff at all levels in the development of meaningful programs for incarcerated mothers and their children. Failure to act will only contribute to the growing cycle of crime in our society.

Joann B. Morton is an associate professor in the College of Criminal Justice at the University of South Carolina.

Deborah M. Williams is a master's candidate at the University of South Carolina.

4

Babies Behind Bars

Programs for Incarcerated Mothers and Pregnant Women

Julie Lays

Abstract

Incarceration can cause severe stress to pregnant women or mothers with small children at home. To prevent this problem, a growing number of states are implementing alternative sentencing programs that allow these women offenders to be reunited with their children and prepare them for reintegration into community life. Aside from these benefits, these programs also ease congestion in prisons and save taxpayers' money. California has been a leader in creating such programs and its officials are pleased with its level of success.

The benefits of keeping mothers and babies together while mom serves time are producing more community-based, alternative programs around the country.

Sandy sold drugs and got caught. Fortunately for her and her child, she lives in California. She is serving her time, with her baby daughter, at the Elizabeth Fry Center in San Francisco. Sandy has earned her high school diploma and has gone through medical assistant's training at the local community college since being accepted in the program. When she's finished serving her time, her daughter will know her, and she'll have a job at the local hospital. "She'll be making more than many of my staff at the center," says Deborah Haffner, director.

Sandy is among the growing number of women incarcerated every year. Due partly to the "war on drugs" thas has changed mandatory sentencing laws, the number of women in state and

Babies behind bars (Programs for incarcerated mothers and pregnant women), by Julie Lays. State Legislatures, May 1992 v 18 n 5 p44 (3). Reprinted by permission.

federal prisons at the end of 1989 was a record 40,556, according to the Bureau of Justice Statistics. (Another 30,299 were in jails.) That's a 200 percent increase since 1980. And whie women still accounted for only 5.7 percent of the nation's prisoners, it's the highest percentage since data collection began in 1926. This rate of growth exceeds that for men in each year since 1981.

For women who come to prison pregnant or with small dependent children at home, the stress on them and their children can be fatal. What happens to them is the focus of more and more alternative sentencing programs for women designed to allow mothers to stay with their children, avoid foster care and return to the community prepared to stay out of trouble. Proponents of these residential care programs say they are also saving taxpayers' money and easing prison overcrowding.

"What all this increased incarceration of women is doing to the family structure and the way it is affecting the next generation," says Gail Smith, executive director of Chicago Legal Aid for Incarcerated Mothers, "makes it--from a taxpayers' perspective--so foolish that we haven't done something about it."

In 1986, most women in prison (42 percent) were there for property offenses. And the percentage of women in prison for drug offenses exceeded that of men. Forty-one percent of the women were in for violent crimes, increasingly for killing their abusive husbands and boyfriends.

More than three-fourths of the women in prison are mothers--young, single mothers with two dependent children at home. They are often undereducated, unskilled, unemployed, poor and hooked on drugs. Ten percent of women prisoners are pregnant.

For the women sentenced while pregnant, health care in prison can be inadequate. Doris was convicted of a parole violation and sentenced to six months in county jail in Oakland, Calif. She was seven months pregnant at the time and addicted to heroin. Instead of receiving methadone treatment, she was forced to withdraw cold turkey. She suffered severe withdrawal, with headaches, abdominal pain, vomiting and diarrhea. When she was eight and one-half months pregnant, she had extreme uterine pain and felt no fetal movements. Three days later her still-born daughter was removed by Cesarean section.

Louwanna was pregnant when convicted of welfare fraud in Bakersfield, Calif. Although she was a low-security prisoner, she was confined for 24 hours a day and forced to sleep on the floor of an overcrowded cell. She was exposed to several contagious diseases, including tuberculosis and measles. She was never seen by an obstetrician. When she went into labor the guards told her that she would have to wait because there was no medical staff available at the time. Three hours later she gave birth outside the door of the clinic. The baby experienced oxygen loss at birth and died several months later.

Critics argue that correctional systems--with taxpayers' money--need not provide better medical care than the women were giving themselves before being convicted. They often do not or cannot. Women, after all, still make up less than 6 percent of the prison population.

"What we've discovered," says Ellen Barry, director of the San Francisco-based Legal Services for Prisoners with Children, "is that prison systems--across the board--have serious deficiencies in their prenatal care." Her organization represented Doris and Louwanna in lawsuits challenging the quality of medical care for pregnant women in those county jails.

For women lucky enough to deliver healthy babies while incarcerated, they must return to their cells 24 to 72 hours after giving birth--without the baby. Mothers must find alternative care for their children, often relatives but sometimes foster care. Many prison systems allow children to visit and may conduct parenting classes, but few allow mothers and children to stay together.

Experts agree it is important for a baby to develop a close attachment to his caretaker early on to ensure emotional, mental and even physical health. Citing Freud, among others, Barbara Bloom, a criminal justice consultant with the National Council on Crime and Delinquentcy, says, "An infant or young child who is prevented from establishing such an attachment may go through a number of stages including active protest, withdrawal from interpersonal relationships and perhaps a complete separation from any effective interaction." She goes on to say that in a study of infants and preschool children of incarcerated mothers the children showed a wide range of unhealthy behavior such as constant crying, little response to stimulation, little effort to crawl and incidents of self-punishment. The incarcerated mother also gives up the choice of whether to breastfeed.

For those women who already have children at home, the separation from them when incarcerated can be devastating. Mothers in prison often face infrequent visits with their children. Relatives or foster parents may be reluctant to allow the children any contact with their incarcerated parents. Or transportation may be a problem, involving long distances from home to the prison. Jails often do not allow physical contact during visits. One toddler, never before apart from her mother, refused to eat and drink and experienced dehydration when not allowed any physical contact with her mother.

Incarcerated mothers also face the threat of loss of parental rights. Nora was sentenced to 18 months in prison for forgery in Illinois. Her 4-year-old daughter DeeAnn, who had never been away

140

from her mother before, was placed in foster care. The foster parent wanted to adopt, and the state filed a petition to terminate Nora's parental rights. The caseworker admitted that DeeAnn wanted to go home to her mother and suffered depression when she couldn't see her. When a psychologist determined that DeeAnn had been sexually abused in the foster home, she was moved to a new home, and the adoption stopped.

Critics argue, though, that women shouldn't be treated differently just because they are pregnant or have small children. Punishment for breaking the law should be administered equally.

But must a child also be punished when his mother breaks the law? "These kids suffer unique hardships," says Bloom, "particularly when they don't have any contact with their moms." If they wind up in the foster care system, they may be bounced around from home to home and separated from their brothers and sisters. They face the stigma of having their mothers in prison. And studies have shown that children of inmates are five times more likely than their peers to be labeled as delinquents.

New York was the first state of address this problem when it established--by law--a prison nursery way back in 1901. Women of all security levels can apply to live in the nursery; babies may stay for a year, or longer, with special permission from the superintendent. Inmates must undergo evaluation of their mental and emotional state, and placement is determined by the best interest of the child. Through the Children's Center at the prison, inmates learn about being parents--from changing diapers to basic nutrition to child development. Babies stay in the nursery, which is staffed by a nurse and several counselors, while their mothers take classes or work.

But do we really want babies in prison nurseries? "I don't think so," says Smith of the Chicago Legal Aid for Incarcerated Mothers. She says prison security and procedures often don't adapt well to sick babies in the middle of the night. "We want them in community-based facilities, where the orientation is child development and family needs," says Smith.

That's what California decided was best when the Legislature passed a bill in 1978 to develop the Mother-Infant Care Program. The program was designed to reunite law-risk, non-violent inmates with their young children (under age 6) in a halfway house setting for the duration of the mother's sentence. Mothers take parenting classes, do community service work and have access to job training and other classes. It took a lawsuit in 1985 to expand the program to its present seven centers housing around 100 women.

"When there are over 6,500 women in state prisons in California, it's ludicrous that we're serving only 100," Haffner says.

Seymour Morgan of the California Department of Corrections, says a major obstacle is finding suitable homes for the centers. "Nobody wants inmates living next door," he says. "These programs make the public uneasy and nervous. Rezoning is very difficult."

San Francisco's Elizabeth Fry Center, a two-story Victorian home, faced strong neighborhood objections. "But the support now is great," says Haffner who had to work hard to convince her neighbors the center would not ruin their middle- to upper-middle class neighborhood or put them in danger. "Foes turned into friends," she says.

After women are screened (no one convicted of violent offenses or found to be an unfit mother by any court is allowed into the program),they are sent to Haffner to be reunited with their children and begin rehabilitation. All 10 women share in household chores and child care. Older kids go to preschools and the women can choose between education or finding a job. There are schools and transportation near by. Parenting classes are required. "Learning to live together and get along is part of the challenge," says Haffner. "It's kind of like dorm life."

Carrie came to the program when her son was a baby. She had been kicked out of her parents' house when she was in junior high school and had lived on the streets since then. She had an alcohol problem that ended when she killed someone in a traffic accident. Though it is very unusual for someone convicted of vehicular homicide to be accepted into one of the programs, Carrie was. By the time she was released, she had earned her real estate license and was hired by her father. She is now working at Hewlett-Packard, and her son is in a Head Start program.

California is viewed as the leader of these residential, alternative programs, but it is not the only state where they exist. Massachusetts' Houston House serves 15 pregnant women who have been incarcerated at the Massachusetts Correctional Institution-Framingham. Pregnant women within 18 months of parole are transferred to Houston House for intensive perinatal care and alcohol or drug addiction treatment. It works with a nearby hospital to prove medical care for high-risk, difficult pregnancies. By the time the women leave the program, they have found affordable housing, gotten a job or enrolled in training and know about community treatment services. During the year following their release, Houston House staff continue to provide support, including continuing recovery services, assistance with family re-unification and medical care.

Summit House, with some funding from the North Carolina legislature, provides similar services to pregnant women and mothers

142

in Guilford County, N.C. Women take courses in interpersonal, parenting and practical skills. These include problem solving, anger control, cooking, housekeeping and budgeting. Children up to age 7 can live with their mothers in the house and receive family counseling, education and health care.

Critics argue that these programs are too cushy for law breakers. Although most programs are kept secure with 24-hour supervision, alarm systems, urine tests and random room searches, they do allow felons the freedom to work and go to school.

Do these programs work? "Any program that helps to maintain the mother's tie with her children," says Bloom "while giving her parenting education, dealing with her substance abuse problem, preparing her for employment and connecting her with community resources, puts her in a far better position when released than those released straight out of prison."

Barry says the California program has been shown to be successful. She says statistics show that women in the program have a 20 percent lower recidivism rate than women who are incarcerated. Haffner claims an 84 percent success rate at the Fry Center. (Those women, of course, may be more successful at staying out of trouble because they were screened for the program and finished it. Twenty-five percent drop out of the program and return to prison.) Maintaining ties with her family is what some criminal justice experts say keeps the woman offender from coming back to prison.

Besides easing prison overcrowding, exacerbated by a 200 percent increase in incarceration rates, the programs save money. "What we are spending to incarcerate the mother in what is, in effect, a maximum-security prison, plus foster care for her kids--which is not doing the children any great favors--is so much more than it costs to run small, community-based facilities," says Smith. Although the actual operating costs of keeping a women in a community-based home is not a lot less than keeping her in prison, the other benefits make it worthwhile. The programs are cost-effective, says Barry, if you factor in that they also can prevent recidivism, foster care, medical problems for the baby and mother, and future delinquents.

"It really is to everybody's benefit," says Smith, "because there's nothing that's more likely to make a woman angry and upset and feel like lashing out than out knowing what's going on with her kids."

5

Developing Correctional Facilities for Female Juvenile Offenders: Design and Programmatic Considerations

Shelly Zavlek
Rebecca Maniglia

G irls represent a challenge for the juvenile justice system. Their unique needs have to be considered in all aspects of facility design and operations. While much work has been done to explain what female-responsive programming looks like in a variety of settings, little has been done to explain how that programming might affect the design of juvenile residential facilities themselves. This article on female juvenile offenders is an effort to show how the programmatic needs of girls can translate into design concepts for more effective and responsive girls facilities and is based on a review of research as well as the authors' first-hand experience and interviews with staff and residents of juvenile correctional facilities.

GIRLS IN THE JUVENILE JUSTICE SYSTEM

Juvenile Arrest Trends

From the mid-1980s to the mid-1990s, there was a precipitous increase in the overall number of juvenile arrests. However, the 10-year trend in rising juvenile crime appeared to have reached a plateau by the mid-1990s, and the number of arrests began to decline by

Developing correctional Facilities by Shelly Zavlek, Rebecca Maniglia in Corrections Today; v69 i4 p58. Reprinted with permission of the American Correctional Association, Alexandria, VA. Endnotes have been removed.

1997. According to FBI data, there was a 25 percent decrease in the overall number of juvenile arrests each year from 1996 to 2000. During that period, while the total number of juveniles arrested each year decreased by 25 percent, the number of females arrested decreased by only 11 percent. Although overall juvenile arrests have remained fairly constant since 2000, the number of female juveniles arrested has steadily increased. Whereas females under the age of 18 made up 25 percent of all juveniles arrested in 1996, they made up 30 percent of juveniles arrested in 2004--and that percentage has been increasing every year since 1996.

Female and Male Juvenile Offenses

Arrest numbers alone do not tell the whole story. They do not reflect the tremendous disparity between the nature of offenses for which female and male juveniles are arrested and institutionalized. In November 2005, the Annie E. Casey Foundation released a report by Francine Sherman titled Detention Reform and Girls: Challenges and Solutions, which examined data on the detention of girls from 1990 through 2001. According to the report, the number of girls entering juvenile detention nationwide rose 50 percent between 1990 and 1999, compared with only a 4 percent increase for boys.

Girls are far more likely than boys to be detained for misdemeanors, technical violations of probation and parole, and status offenses such as underage drinking or curfew violations that would not be crimes if committed by an adult, the report notes. Nationwide, girls represented 19 percent of the young people detained in 2001 but account for 24 percent of those detained specifically for technical violations and 43 percent of those detained for status offenses. The report suggests that, contrary to the statutory purposes of detention, many jurisdictions are detaining girls not simply to maintain public safety, but to protect and arrange services for girls who have not committed serious crimes--including many who have run away from chaotic or abusive homes.

While the current situation requires a number of solutions, the remainder of this article focuses on the secure facilities designed to house female juveniles--specifically on how the programmatic needs of girls can translate into design concepts for more effective and responsive girls facilities.

COMMONALITIES OF FEMALE JUVENILE OFFENDERS

While there are many standard considerations (including safety, security and cost) that impact the design of secure juvenile facilities, programming and space purpose also should shape facility design. Therefore, in order to consider the design implications of the female juvenile population, one must first understand the issues facing this population and the key elements of a female-responsive program.

The past 10 years have seen research that has expanded and confirmed the early academic work of pioneers such as Meda Chesney-Lind, Joanne Belknap and others in articulating the needs of girls and young women. Whether using national, state or local populations, a reliable list of needs and key issues arise again and again for this population. The fact that these issues vary by location, age, socioeconomic class and race/ethnicity has resulted in the creation of standard recommendations for female-responsive services.

Sexual, physical and/or emotional victimization are among the most important commonalities found in populations of girls and young women involved in juvenile justice. For instance, in their 1998 study of girls in California, the National Council on Crime and Delinquency (NCCD) identified victimization, primarily sexual abuse, as the most critical pathway to female delinquency for young girls. The report indicated that 92 percent of the girls interviewed reported a history of physical, sexual and/or emotional abuse. Likewise, citing other studies that found girls were as much as three times more likely than boys to have been sexually abused, the Office of Juvenile Justice and Delinquency Prevention's (OJJDP) Guiding Principles for Promising Female Programming identified victimization as a key issue for juvenile female offenders. State studies have identified similar concerns. Studies also show a connection between depression and involvement in criminal activity. In a report entitled Adolescent Girls: The Role of Depression in the Development of Delinquency, the National Institute of Justice asserts that "57 percent of mildly to moderately depressed girls engaged in higher levels of aggressive behavior, compared with only 13 percent of those who were not depressed."

Research conducted by NCCD also identifies family fragmentation, academic failure, and health and mental health issues as some of the greatest concerns for girls and young at-risk women. The American Bar Association's report Justice by Gender affirmed the work of earlier research in identifying critical concerns that programmatic solutions must address: family problems, victimization both inside and outside the formal juvenile justice system, health and mental health issues, and school failure. OJJDP publications since the mid-1990s have made similar claims, citing substance abuse, teen pregnancy, academic failure, mental health needs, gang membership and societal pressure as issues of concern for this population, and academic studies have confirmed this standard list.

FEMALE-RESPONSIVE PROGRAMMING

Generally it can be said that in a female-responsive program all aspects of the specific service-delivery system (and the larger system in which it operates) are designed through a female-responsive lens. Practitioners, therefore, make an intentional effort to understand the shifting literature on female identity and development and use this information when designing specific program elements and general service-delivery systems. In essence, all policy and program development is examined to ensure that it meets the specific and varied gender and cultural needs of girls and young women.

The five female-responsive values, developed for the National Institute of Corrections as part of its training efforts for juvenile female offenders, define the theoretical framework in which female-responsive services exist. Generally it is believed that if these conditions are not present, a program or service delivery system cannot, in good conscience, call itself female-responsive. The following five female-responsive values, therefore, set a high standard by which services delivered to girls and young women ought to be evaluated. Female-responsive services are:

1) Inclusive. Movements of gender equality have historically focused on gender as the primary social category to be addressed. This has resulted in criticisms that the conceptions of gender around which advocacy takes place are those of the majority population. Thus, women's movements have become defined around the needs and desires of white, middle class, heterosexual women and have ignored the unique circumstances of women of color, women living in poverty, and bisexual or lesbian women.

Likewise, the female-responsive services movement has been envisioned by some as focusing exclusively on the issues emerging from gender. However, in their intended form, female-responsive services allow girls and young women to understand gender, race, sexual orientation, socioeconomic class, religion, and other social categories and individual life experiences as all interconnecting to shape their self-identity. Therefore, female-responsive services seek to integrate treatment approaches in ways that allow for multiple perspectives and that encourage advocacy concerning all forms of oppression.

2) Relational. It has been said that "relationships are the glue that holds girls lives together." It is often in the context of relationships that girls define their own self-identity--looking to others' perceptions when shaping their own ideas about the world.

The relational aspects of female delinquency and crime are well-known and documented. Girls often experience delinquency and crime collectively; for example, by shoplifting as a group or engaging in violent physical encounters with one another. Therefore, female-responsive programming acknowledges the role that relationships play in the development of healthy life skills. Typically girls are better able than boys to accept accountability for their harmful actions to others and to confront the emotional and physical difficulties they have experienced in their own interpersonal relationships when they are given the opportunity to connect relationally with service providers.

3) Restorative. Restorative justice practices have become popular in state juvenile justice systems in recent years, with many adopting new practices for handling crime and punishment. The roots of restorative-justice theory can be found in the practices of indigenous peoples throughout the world, as well as in the early forms of criminal justice practiced in Europe. In contemporary justice understandings, however, restorative justice focuses on a philosophical belief that crime should be redefined as harm done to specific victims (including a community) rather than as a violation of arbitrary state laws that identify particular behavior as criminal. Therefore, the proper response to crime is restoration of the damage done. Victims receive compensation, and offenders may be restored through the process of making amends--often both emotionally, through the expression of remorse, and materially, through restitution or community service.

For girls and young women, adopting a female-responsive philosophy means both allowing them the opportunity to experience meaningful accountability to their victims and restore their own broken relationships. Therefore, programmatically responding to the high rates of victimization among girls is as critical as helping them develop empathy skills and opportunities for restitution. While a program may choose not to use all of the formal mechanisms of restorative justice, it should be operating under the basic philosophy that crime and treatment are, in essence, about broken relationships that need restoration.

4) Aware of the social context. All girls and young women receive social pressure based on the societal expectations related to their gender. This social pressure can be further complicated by a young

148

woman's membership in an additional social category of individuals who experience oppression, such as those based on race or ethnicity, sexual orientation, religion, or socioeconomic class. While female-responsive services do not believe that society is the sole cause of the individual behaviors of girls, there is an assumption that the social pressure girls experience does influence their own self-perception. Therefore, female-responsive services attempt to assist girls in becoming critical consumers of media and other forms of social influence, while at the same time creating environments that offer alternatives.

5) Multileveled. The systems of which girls and young women are a part exist within a specific historical context that shapes the choices and quality of the services delivered. For instance, the juvenile justice system has historically created programs designed to serve the needs of its majority (and most violent) population, boys and young men. This has resulted in girls having access only to programming that has been designed for this separate and distinct population. Thus, those involved in the development and delivery of female-responsive services must confront systemic environments and system policies that hinder the ability to assist girls and young women in the work that they need to accomplish.

FEMALE-RESPONSIVE FACILITY DESIGN

An important aspect of designing a facility for girls is acknowledging the specific requirements of female-responsive programming. The past experiences and current needs of girls--and how these are addressed by residential programming--have critical facility design implications.

While it may be true that there are certain design features that are appropriate and useful for all juvenile facilities, there are hidden issues specific to the gender of the population housed. For instance, both male and female juvenile offenders need "structure, education, training and support to succeed," yet how each of these is manifested in the structural design and atmosphere of a facility can vary with the population served. The information provided below aims to address the ways in which aspects of facility design might be affected by gender. The remainder of this section, discusses how secure juvenile residential facilities can be designed to be more responsive to and effective for girls.

Safety, Security and Safe Places

Security and safety are of paramount importance in a correctional system. Efforts should be directed toward preventing any breach of security that might endanger staff, juveniles, visitors or members of the surrounding community. Safety is maintained in accordance with modern standards and guidelines established by state and local agencies responsible for such planning. Further, architectural elements, including grilles, registers, fittings and all fixtures in areas accessible to residents, particularly bedrooms and bathrooms, should be suicide-resistant. Most suicides and suicide attempts take place in bedrooms and bathrooms where youths may be alone without direct supervision for intervals of time.

For girls, these efforts to create physical safety are paramount. However, efforts must also extend to ensuring emotional and cultural safety. In a female-responsive program, one of the most important safety and security tools any facility has is the quality of relationships--relationships among staff, between girls and staff, and among the girls. Therefore, meeting girls' relational needs through policies and physical space that allow for healthy and safe connections is a first step in making a facility safe for girls.

Physical and emotional safety also are affected by the high rates of victimization found in the juvenile female population. Many, if not most, girls in a correctional facility will have suffered sexual and/or physical abuse prior to entering the facility, creating an environment where feeling safe is an important prerequisite to being able to work on treatment issues. Facility staff, therefore, should understand that "the prison system often contributes to the revictimization of these women by perpetuating feelings of powerlessness and vulnerability." Procedures such as restraints, strip searches and intrusive explorations of body parts further exacerbate feelings of victimization by presenting a threat of further sexual assaults. Policies and procedures that reflect this knowledge should be adopted. For example the manner in which security procedures are conducted should be modified so that they are not disem-powering.

Other related implications are important for facility design. Whenever possible, private interview rooms should be available for intake questioning, which typically includes questions about sexual behavior and abuse. Moreover, close attention should be paid to the placement of windows and vision panels in the area where body searches are performed.

Privacy

Opaque shower curtains in front of multiple single shower units and saloon doors on bathrooms satisfy privacy needs without compromising institutional security. Girls can be made to feel that there is something giving them privacy from the watchful eyes of staff, while giving staff the ability to observe what they must for security reasons.

Although providing natural lighting is critical, it must be achieved while being sensitive to privacy needs when designing for girls. Providing appropriate covering for bedroom windows allows for privacy and yet does not eliminate natural light or prohibit staff monitoring of girls while in their rooms. For example, bedroom windows that face courtyards or other areas that are accessible to youth or to the public may have diffused or obscured glazing that allows light into the room but blocks visual access from the outside. This is especially important if the facility is one of a number of buildings located on a coed campus.

Sightlines and Visibility

The internal layout of a juvenile facility should provide for maximum visibility and supervision, with minimal reliance on electronic surveillance or security escort. Blind spots must be avoided as much as possible throughout the facility. Although closed circuit TV could be used to monitor certain areas, it is important that staff have a direct line of sight to as much of the facility as possible to allow ease of movement and visual supervision. Further, the design of any office and/or program spaces in, or adjacent to, the housing pods should have vision panels that allow for indirect visual supervision of youths by office staff.

Issues of visibility are of particular importance to girls and young women because they are often at risk of self-harming behaviors such as self-mutilation. Girls may also be at risk of exploitation by staff members. Enhanced visibility assists both in reducing staff opportunities for inappropriate contact and in reducing staff's risk of having false charges filed against them. For these reasons, it may also be undesirable to rely on the use of isolation rooms or small segregation units, which are often supervised by a single staff member.

Electronic Technology

Electronic technology may be used in a facility to enhance security and surveillance but must not be substituted for direct staff supervision. Dependence on electronic systems, monitors and closed circuit TV within the facility should be minimized. Some areas, such as sleeping and recreation areas, cannot be adequately supervised without the presence of a staff member.

Given the relational nature of girls and their particular issues of safety and security, technology can never replace the importance of staff on the floor interacting and participating in the program model. For instance, if a staff-duty office is created, it should not be used as a break room for staff or a place to watch girls from a distance, nor should it be positioned so as to encourage such activity. Whenever possible, there should be no staff-duty office on the housing unit for direct-care staff. In order to know what is going on in any population of girls, and to ensure effective supervision in high-risk situations, it is important that staff are with the girls in the day room during activities. The use of isolation for security or safety issues is not necessarily effective, given girls' need for connection. It is far better in situations of suicide risk, self-harm risk and aggressive acting-out risk to have a staff member stay close by a girl, whether or not she chooses to interact with that staff person.

Relationships

Honoring the relationships a juvenile brings into a facility and allowing her to create healthy and meaningful relationships with facility staff is a key element of any program. Whether it is family, friends or the community, young women thrive in an environment where they are able to tend to the relationships in their lives and even form new ones. For this reason, whenever possible, states should build smaller, locally based facilities that allow juveniles to be kept close to their families and community support systems.

Community-based programming allows for the facility to bring in outside resources for staff training, program development and direct-service delivery. Agencies such as sexual assault centers and domestic-violence shelters can be vital resources to a female-responsive residential program, and this kind of networking is enhanced when facilities are not geographically isolated.

Placing female juveniles in a facility that is in close proximity to their homes, families and community support networks also helps to ease subsequent reintegration to the outside community. Removing girls from their communities for placement in a remote facility not only breaks the ties these girls need with their families and support networks, it disrupts the chain of services and relationships that they have with counselors, therapists and other staff with whom they are involved in the local community. Although this is important for all juveniles, many of the risk factors for girls and young women originate in the home; therefore, involving the family and a girl's community as part of the recovery is an important element of treatment and rehabilitation.

This respect for relationships in a gendered context has many important implications for facility design. The design of the housing pods should encourage interaction between staff and juveniles, ensuring that the day room is an integral part of the housing pod. Movable furniture can help encourage relationship building by providing a setting conducive to small groups and intimate interactions between staff and girls and by creating a dayroom where people feel comfortable having personal conversations.

Many juvenile female offenders are also teen mothers. They are, in essence, raising the next generation, even while they are being held in the facility. Therefore, designing family visiting rooms with child-sized chairs and toys and supplying spaces where mothers and their children can interact in a positive and healthy environment will strengthen this vital relationship. The room should be large enough to accommodate visitors and ensure privacy for families who wish to talk about difficult issues with facility staff. Such spaces need to have access to restroom facilities with baby changing tables for families. However, it should be noted that many families are suspicious of juvenile justice efforts to include them because these efforts often have ulterior motives associated with blame, issue identification or abuse disclosure. This needs to be taken into consideration when using spaces intended to encourage familial interaction.

The need to honor relationships also has implications for the design of facility living spaces for girls. Anecdotal information suggests that double occupancy rooms can be beneficial to girls by allowing them to cultivate a new and important relationship and by giving the occupants a better sense of community. However, double rooms also can create unsafe environments for girls, so any decisions about room occupancy must take place within the context of other efforts to ensure safety and security.

Normative Environments

All juveniles should be provided the opportunity to be in the least restrictive, appropriate environment. Since the majority of juveniles in the system are nonviolent, creating an environment that is as close as possible to a real-world setting makes sense. Furthermore, housing youths in a facility they must care for and respect keeps them from lapsing into the bad habits anticipated by a more institutional, security-grade environment. Using ordinary carpets and furnishings as well as a residential color palette--resembling a college dorm--allows the building to be used as a tool for teaching responsibility and provides a positive environment for treatment.

The furnishings and fixtures must be durable, easy to maintain, and appropriate for a secure residential facility. Dayrooms should contain movable tables and chairs with sufficient mass/weight to avoid their use as a weapon--or light enough to be harmless if used in such a manner. Natural light is also important in maintaining a rehabilitative environment and should be provided in each bedroom and program space, while still maintaining safety and security.

Some jurisdictions have determined that, for the majority of the population in their care, security hardware (which is very expensive) is unnecessary. In many facilities, recreation yards are located in central courtyards surrounded by buildings; there are no barbed wire or razor wire fences, no traditional security locks and no traditional cells. Housing units may contain a combination of single-occupancy, double-occupancy and/or dormitory-style sleeping areas. These areas may have features such as free-standing beds and desks (which, depending on the population, may be fixed in place), security-grade marker boards for personal notes or pictures, a mirror, and space for personal effects. Private or shared bathrooms should, where possible, be placed in the common area of the housing unit.

Creating a female-friendly environment means, when possible, achieving all of the recommended elements, while adding little touches that make the living environment feel more like a home. This can be accomplished by adding design features such as curtains to windows. The design of girls housing units might also include attention to details such as additional sinks, toilets, mirrors, and outlets for equipment such as blow dryers or curling irons, and adjusting the height of equipment or door handles. Creating larger grooming areas with amenities such as bathtubs can also be important.

Another way to make the environment more comforting is by providing dayrooms with bookcases and appropriate reading materials that include a wide array of books on female issues and women's fiction (particularly including those written by African-American and Latino women). Also, including security-grade bulletin boards in bedrooms can be an outlet for self expression.

Further, since many of the girls have suffered feelings of powerlessness due to their victimization, granting them some control of their environment--such as being able to turn the light switches on

154

and off (with appropriate overrides)--can provide a good tool for empowerment and rehabilitation.

Programming spaces and learning environments. Residential facility design usually requires that space serve multiple purposes. Classrooms, multipurpose rooms and program spaces should be flexible to accommodate a variety of activities and teaching methods. Classroom design should accommodate individualized programming to meet the needs of students at varying academic levels.

Educational programming spaces should offer a stimulating learning environment for academic learning and vocational training. They should include adequate security-grade display cabinets and bulletin boards to display students' work. Noise reduction and natural light are also very important, with calming colors being used whenever possible.

In a coed facility, it is not unusual for facility classrooms to contain only one or two girls per class. Therefore, providing teachers with direct visual access to all areas of the classroom, as well as space for girls to sit separately or near adult staff, will ensure that girls are safe in the school environment.

It also is important to include space where females can talk and learn about female development and health issues with a level of confidentiality and where they can gather written information on issues such as pregnancy, sexually transmitted diseases, contraception and overall female health. The design of medical exam rooms is also critical because gynecological exams can cause many girls to relive issues of victimization. These rooms should be private and should not contain cameras. They should have appropriate medical exam tables and equipment used exclusively by a female nurse practitioner whenever possible.

A specific facility feature that needs to be adjusted for female offenders is the type of food served. "Female offenders are fed the same meals as their male counterparts--equal in calorie count, carbohydrates and sugars." Such a diet often contributes to weight gain and may have negative health impacts, including development or exacerbation of eating disorders. Something as simple as adding a salad bar to the eating facility can have a significant positive impact on females. It also is important to work with a nutritionist to develop a menu specifically for girls.

CONCLUSION

The issues surrounding female offenders in the justice system are complex, and the research is clear on certain matters. Most young females entering the juvenile justice system are victims of abuse and require a healing and safe environment. Most enter the system for nonviolent offenses, and up to one-third for status-type offenses. Relationships are critical to these young females. Therefore, whenever possible, it is essential to include family and other significant relationships in the development of treatment plans and as part of the treatment process. Program elements such as mentors who can relate to the girls' experiences and opportunities for girls to develop relationships of trust and interdependence with other women already present in their lives (such as friends, relatives, neighbors, church members) are essential for effective gender-specific programming for adolescent females. Each of these programmatic needs of girls can translate into design concepts for more effective and responsive girls facilities. It is evident that jurisdictions should make careful choices when designing or converting facilities for female juveniles.

Shelley Zavlek, J.D., M.S.Ed., is president of Justice Solutions Group in Closter, N.J. Rebecca Maniglia, Ph.D., is an assistant professor in the Department of Criminal Justice and Criminology at Northern Arizona University.

Part 5

Serious Juvenile
Offenders

1

Childhood Predictors of Adult Criminality: A Meta-Analysis Drawn from the Prospective Longitudinal Literature

Alan Leschied
Debbie Chiodo
Elizabeth Nowicki
Susan Rodger

Author's Abstract

Sufficient research now exists in the psychology of criminal conduct literature to address the long-term impact of early childhood and adolescent experiences on later adult outcomes. In the present meta-analysis, selected studies were prospective and longitudinal, tracking a variety of early childhood and family factors that could potentially predict later involvement in the adult criminal justice system. Thirty-eight studies met the selection criteria. Major findings indicate that dynamic versus static predictors are related to later adult criminal justice involvement. The older the child was at the time the predictor was measured, the stronger was the relationship to adult offending. Within the set of dynamic predictors, childhood and adolescent factors that rate most highly include a variety of behavioural concerns including early identification of aggression, attentional problems, motor restlessness, and attention seeking. Emotional concerns consistent with depression including withdrawal, anxiety, self-deprecation, and social alienation are also represented.

Childhood predictors of adult criminality: A meta-analysis drawn from the prospective longitudinal literature (Canada), by Alan Leschied, Debbie Chiodo, Elizabeth Nowicki and Susan Roger. (2008). Canadian Journal of Criminology and Criminal Justice July 2008, v50, i4, p435 (33). www.ccja-acjp.can/en. Reprinted by permission of University of Toronto Press Incorporated. References and study characteristic summary have been removed.

160

Predictors also included family descriptors such as a variety of
negative parenting strategies including coerciveness, authoritarian
behaviours, lack of child supervision, and family structure variables
such as witnessing violence, inter-parental conflict, family stressors,
and poor communication. Results are discussed in relation to
prevention strategies for targeted services that influence the
probability of antisocial outcomes for children into adulthood.

N umerous commentaries have appeared, particularly over the
past ten years, noting the important contributions of
developmental criminology in adding to both our theoretical
and practical understanding of the life course of crime for children
and adolescents that can continue into adulthood. Farrington (1997)
suggests that an understanding of developmental constructs in the
context of criminal behaviour contributes to an appreciation of the
interaction and implications of life events at different ages that have
certain predictable outcomes, characterized as factors that either
relate to desistance or exacerbation of antisocial behaviour. Le Blanc
and Loeber (1998) suggest that "the application of developmental
perspectives to the study of offending is likely to advance current
understanding of offending's causes and courses" (115-116).

The implications of such a developmental appreciation of
life course trajectories can contribute considerably to our
understanding of the effectiveness of prevention and intervention. A
social developmental framework that integrates the major theoretical
orientations of our current psychologically informed understanding
of criminal behaviour, personal, familial, and structural variables can
be identified that can guide the understanding of both "causal and
mediating processes hypothesized to predict behavior over the course
of development" (Andrews and Bonta 2007, 95). Farrington and
Welsh (2007) more recently suggest that a social developmental
framework can guide the selection of risk-focused targets in
prevention and intervention.

Coincidentally, while social developmental theory has
contributed to an understanding of life course trajectories for
antisocial behaviour, a number of longitudinal studies have appeared
reporting on empirical findings related to the early life experiences
for children and youth and their relationship to adult antisocial
outcomes. Such data are a critical part of theory building related to
risk prediction and can enhance viewing risk as a construct based on
longitudinal studies within a developmental framework. This area,
referred to as developmental criminology, holds the potential for
refining our understanding of how risk factors may work at different
ages and stages within the lives of children and their families to

predict offending into the adult years. The present meta-analysis drew on the prospective, longitudinal literature in child development in identifying childhood and youth predictors for later adult offending.

LITERATURE REVIEW

Longitudinal studies now report on the link between early child experience and subsequent antisocial behaviour. These findings suggest that parental inability to foster self-control in their children, neuropsychological disorders, a variety of negative parenting practices, coercive family interactions, and an inability of children to develop age-appropriate social skills (Lacourse, Cote, Nagin, Vitaro, Brendgen, and Tremblay 2002) appear promising in providing a basis for planning for prevention. The research on developmental disorders in children has reflected a range of findings from viewing children in isolation to understanding the impact of the social contexts that contribute to a child's potential for risk. Current findings from the longitudinal literature suggest that certain childhood disorders such as in the development of antisocial orientation will have different developmental trajectories, influenced by different systemic variables (Silk, Nath, Seigel, and Kendall 2000). And while Loeber and Farrington (2000: 746) suggest that "[t]he majority of childhood disorders reflect age normative problem behaviors which most children give up as they grow up," the challenge for developmental researchers is to identify which behaviours identified early in childhood are not transient developmental reactions but rather relate to later difficulty. Within the criminogenic risk context, early warning signs of protracted difficulty identified by a number of researchers suggest that such childhood factors as temperament, impulsivity, social withdrawal, aggression and hyperactivity associated with disruptive behaviour, family-based factors reflecting poor parenting practices, low supervision, physical punishment, neglect and poor communication, age, and gender (Loeber and Farrington; Hanish and Guerra 2002; Lacourse et al. 2002; Moffitt, Caspi, Harrington, and Milne 2002) all are factors that can play a role in the early prediction of later criminal conduct.

RELEVANCE OF THEORY

Social developmental theory can assist in creating a conceptual framework for identifying appropriate targets for intervention. For example, therapeutic progress is more likely to occur when theory is emphasized in intervention (Conduct Problems Prevention Group 2002; Kazdin 1997). In addition, as emphasized in the risk-predication literature by Andrews and Bonta (2007), a differential understanding of disorders that are influenced by dynamic over static characteristics and the timing or influence of systemic factors that can differentially affect childhood and adolescent outcomes will provide critical input to the understanding of prevention and early intervention.

The science of criminal conduct is now mature to the point where sufficient studies exist reporting on the long-term outcomes for children who experience early disruptions that can lead to later persistent involvement in both the youth and adult criminal justice systems. While small relative to the cross-sectional literature related to risk, the number of longitudinal studies is now adequate such that general findings drawn together through meta-analysis can provide policy makers, practitioners, and researchers with important findings on the identification of factors placing children and youth at risk. The importance of testing the predictive adequacy of early childhood experience within such a methodological framework lies in the increased reliability and validity of findings based on longitudinal studies. Acknowledging the contributions of meta-analysis, particularly within the criminal justice literature (Lipsey and Wilson 1998), this meta-analysis drew on the prospective longitudinal literature in risk prediction to examine static and dynamic risk factors that relate to children and youth who progress into the adult criminal justice system.

METHOD

Studies were identified relating predictors of criminogenic risk for youths to their eighteenth birthday, or the age of majority, in determining entry into the adult criminal justice system in the country where the study took place. Only studies that were prospective and longitudinal were included. This is a methodological improvement over the use of cross-sectional studies used in most meta-analyses, which are less able to account for previous experiences of the subjects in the studies and how these might affect the findings. Longitudinal studies, particularly where concern is focused on developmental risk, will be more sensitive to within-subject comparisons. Relevant literature both published and unpublished from the major electronic databases was included: Psychinfo, ERIC, Social Work Abstracts, Medline, and Criminal Justice Abstracts. Searches were limited by date of publication from 1994 to 2004--a period during which the major prospective, longitudinal studies have appeared. The population was limited to childhood, school age, and adolescence. If the database did not allow for population limits, the keyword youth was included in each search.

Thirty-seven literature searches were performed on each database. Each search reflected a variation in the combination of 17 keywords: meta-analysis, longitudinal, crime, criminality, criminal, involvement, prediction, predictors, trajectories, risk and risk factors, at risk populations, determinants, delinquency, offending, young offenders, and recidivism. The keywords were selected on the basis of reviews and meta-analyses in the area. Indexed databases that generated keywords for searches were also included. References of each study were reviewed to ensure all relevant studies were reflected by the search. Search terms generated 48 studies of which 38 contained data that were reported in a format that was amenable for the analysis.

CODING OF STUDIES

Prior to statistical analysis, data from the selected studies were coded into categories including authorship and cohort name to ensure non-duplication of the data source. Studies were also coded according to predictor variables that were assigned to one of two major categories: (1) family factors that included static risk, parental mental health, parental management, family structure, and adverse family environment; and (2) child factors including static risk, internalizing, externalizing, social interpersonal, and developmental concerns, child-specific school and learning issues, pro-social behaviour, and criminal history.

For both family and child factors, static risk was defined as one that had occurred in the past and could not be reversed or changed. For family factors this included parents' criminal history and complications during pregnancy; for child factors this included the age of onset of both the child's criminal behaviour and drug use. Dynamic risk characterizes factors in the lives of children/youth that are changeable over time and will be most amenable to intervention. In family factors, this includes parental management; for child factors, dynamic factors include lack of control and truancy.

Adult outcomes for each study were coded for official conviction or self-report. A further category focused on the age of participants prior to reaching the age of majority, and data were coded as early (birth to 6 years), mid (7 to 11 years), or late childhood/adolescence (12 to age of majority).

DEMOGRAPHIC SUMMARY

Sample sizes were summed across the 38 studies reflecting 66,647 participants. There were 43,586 males (65.4%), 19,233 females (28.9%), and 3,828 (5.7%) participants not identified by gender. Half of all participants were from Scandinavian countries (11 = 33,384 or 50.1%), with the next largest group from the United States (11 = 16,455 or 24.7%). Other geographical areas included Denmark (n = 10,459 or 15.7%), Australia and New Zealand (n = 3,247 or 4.9%), Holland (n = 1,452 or 2.2%), and the United Kingdom (n = 1,650 or 2.5%).

The overall mean age at the initial data-tracking assessment was 10.5 years (SD = 5.0). Twenty-five studies provided mean ages, with 13 providing age ranges. In order to calculate an overall mean, the midpoint of each age range was used. The same procedure was used to determine mean age at follow-up (M = 24.6, SD = 5.6) and the average number of years between childhood and adult assessments (M = 13.3, SD = 7.4).

ESTIMATING PROGRAM EFFECTS

Using Comprehensive Meta-analysis (version 2), effect size (ES) estimates were derived from 38 studies. ES was measured as the impact of the independent variable (e.g., behavioural predictor) on the dependent variable (e.g., official conviction). Because the dependent variable is often measured differently from one study to another (e.g., self-report, official convictions, violent versus nonviolent offences), it was necessary to transform the reported data to a common metric (similar to a Z score) before calculating the mean ES. In meta-analytic studies, data are statistically combined to provide an estimated ES, in this case, the impact of a given predictor such as the child's behaviour on a measure of adult criminality. Information was entered according to the categories previously mentioned. ES was entered directly if provided within a study, or was computed after relevant summary data were entered. The program calculated weighted effect sizes and significance, 95% confidence intervals (CI), tests of the null hypotheses, and heterogeneity statistics (Q).

As a general guideline, Cohen (1988) proposed small, medium, and large values for ES. A "medium" ES (0.50) was defined by Cohen to represent an effect likely to be visible to the naked eye of a careful observer. In fact, medium ES approximates the average size of observed effects in various fields. Cohen set a "small" ES (.20) as one that is noticeably smaller than a medium ES but not so small as to be trivial. Finally, a "large" ES (0.80) was described as the same distance above medium as small was below it. While these conventions are useful and a valid way to summarize results, Weisz, Sandler, Durlak, and Anton (2005) argue that proper interpretation of ES values may differ, depending on the particular independent variable examined, and practical significance must always be weighed into the judgment. Thus, in the current meta-analysis, even a statistically "small" ES could be interpreted as having an impact in predicting adult convictions, given that adult convictions in general are relatively low-base-rate phenomena. Effect sizes were calculated in a similar manner for all studies such that positive values always meant that the independent variable (e.g., behavioural concerns) was a predictor of adult criminality. Negative values indicate that the independent variable was a predictor in the control group rather than the experimental group (or for single group studies, prediction was in the opposite direction).

Most studies compared predictors on more than one type of outcome measure. Because multiple ES values derived from the same study may not represent statistically independent observations, multiple ES values obtained from individual measures within the same study were averaged to obtain a single ES for the outcomes.

RESULTS

Results are presented in five sections: descriptive characteristics of the studies, overall meta-analysis across all outcomes and predictors for child factors, separate analyses for each child predictor, an overall meta-analysis across all outcomes and predictors for family factors, and separate analyses for each family predictor. Reported results are for a random effects analysis, which is appropriate as a result of the recognized variability within the sampling of studies (Borenstein and Rothstein 1999). Weighted effect sizes are reported for all analyses, since this approach gives greater weight to ES values from larger samples. It has been suggested that, where possible, weighted ES values are preferable to unweighted calculations, where ES values are given equal weight, regardless of the sample size (Wolfe 1986).

OVERALL EFFECT OF ALL OUTCOMES AND PREDICTORS FOR CHILD FACTORS

The 29-study database of child factor studies yielded 274 ES measurements (see Tables 1 and 2). Child factors included static risk (e.g., age, gender), internalizing concerns (e.g., depressive symptoms, anxiety), externalizing concerns (e.g., aggression, antisocial behaviour), social and interpersonal concerns (e.g., social skills), developmental concerns (e.g., speech and motor development), and school/ learning child-specific concerns (e.g., academic achievement). The weighted overall ES across all mean ES measurements was calculated. Overall, the child predictors examined by this synthesis appear to modestly predict adult criminality. Regardless of the type of child factor examined, the overall ES was

.29 (CI = .17-.40), which is significant ([Z.sub.c] = 4.93, p < .001). This suggests that child factors in general have a modest effect in predicting adult correctional outcomes.

The highly heterogeneous nature of the distribution suggests large differential effects across studies ([Q.sub.t] = 242.52, df=28, p<.001). These findings are not surprising, given the varied methodologies reported across studies, the differences in the measurement of predictors, and the heterogeneous nature of the samples. Thus, any attempt to interpret the overall average ES may be misleading, and hence a closer examination of factors that may moderate the ES is warranted.

Two potential sources of variation in ES values across studies were the type of child predictor measured and the age at which the factors were measured. While gender would have been an obvious source of variation, most studies were conducted on males (n = 17, 59%) and of those studies that examined both genders (n = 12), few of these studies included female participants in the analyses because often there were too few subjects to examine statistically.

CHILDHOOD RISK FACTORS

Overall, the findings related to child factors showed that the older the child was displaying a risk factor, the more reliable the factor was in predicting an adult criminogenic outcome. The child factors measured during early childhood (age range = birth to six years) were not significant predictors of adult criminality ([Z.sub.c] = 1.84, p >.05). The ES for all child factors measured during mid-childhood (age range = 7-11 years) predicting adult criminality was .18 (CI = .01-.36), which was significant ([Z.sub.c] = 2.09, p<.05). This is suggestive of a small ES. In contrast, the ES for child factors measured during adolescence (age range = 12 years and older) was .40 (CI = .25-.55), which was significant ([Z.sub.c] = 5.22, p<.001). An ES of this magnitude is noteworthy, suggesting overall that the child factors measured during adolescence are strong and reliable predictors of adult criminality.

ANALYSIS BY CHILD PREDICTOR

The overall analyses examining all child risk factors show that, regardless of the type of predictor examined (e.g., internalizing or externalizing concerns), on average these factors modestly predict adult criminality. It is, however, more meaningful to examine individual child factors that relate to predicting adult correctional outcomes. These individual predictors are divided between static and dynamic predictors.

Static Risk

As mentioned, child static risk includes predictors that are historical and cannot be changed, and include variables such as race, gender, and the age at which the child began engaging in crime and drug use. Regardless of the age at which the static risk predictors were measured (i.e., early childhood, mid-childhood, or adolescence), the overall ES was not significant ([Z.sub.c] = .53, p > .1). Although early initiation of violent and criminal behaviour has been associated with more serious and chronic violent behaviour (e.g., Farrington 1995), there were only two studies (Benda, Corwyn, and Toombs 2001; Eklund and Klinteberg 2003) included in this analysis examining this relationship. Age of onset in regards to the nature of offending has been studied most extensively in the area of risk prediction, and there substantial evidence suggests that those most at risk for adult antisocial behaviour are those with early age onset antisocial behaviour. It is therefore premature to suggest these factors are not reliable predictors of adult criminality on the basis of only two studies and the previous available evidence. Criminal history factors such as prior incarcerations, type of crime, or number of victims were measured only in adolescence. The results of this analysis indicate that the ES for criminal history factors was .38 (CI = .07-.69), which was significant ([Z.sub.c] = 2.4, p < .02).

Dynamic Risk

These risk factors, as outlined earlier, include factors in the lives of children/youth that are changeable over time and will be most amenable to intervention. The strongest associations were identified with behavioural concerns across all age groupings, where the ES was .39 (CI = .16-.62; [Z.sub.c] = 3.36, p<.01). The ES for externalizing concerns (e.g., lack of control, antisocial behaviour) measured in early childhood was .20 (CI = .1-.3; [Z.sub.c] = 3.81, p < .001). This suggests that the externalizing concerns measured during early childhood in this review are a satisfactory predictor of adult criminality, as they are in mid-childhood, with an ES of .31 (CI = .03-.59), and adolescence, with an ES of .52 (CI = .14-.90). These behavioural predictors reflect a variety of concerns including hyperactivity, aggression, and conduct disorder. Internalizing concerns, including depressive symptoms and anxiety, during childhood and adolescence are a modest predictor, where the ES was .22 (CI = .009-.43; [Z.sub.c] = 2.04, p < .05). No significant outcomes were associated with social and interpersonal concerns, developmental disorders, or school-related problems.

OVERALL EFFECT OF ALL OUTCOMES AND PREDICTORS FOR FAMIILY FACTORS

The 19-study database of family factor studies yielded 188 ES measurements (see Table 3). Family factors included static risk (e.g., mother's age at the time of the child's birth), parental mental health (e.g., substance use), parental management (e.g., supervision, discipline), family structure (e.g., size of the family, family separation), and adverse family environment (e.g., family conflict, abuse, neglect). The weighted overall ES across all mean ES measurements was calculated. Overall, the family predictors examined by this synthesis modestly predict adult criminality. Regardless of the type of family factor examined, the overall ES was .25 (CI = .14-.35; [Z.sub.c] = 4.7, p<.001). This suggests that family factors in general have a modest effect in predicting adult criminality. Although the overall mean ES in the current analysis provides evidence that the family predictors were, on average, modest predictors of adult criminality, the nature of the distribution suggests some differential effects across studies ([Q.sub.t] = 98.38, df = 19, p < .001), although this variation was much less, compared to the child factor studies. Again, this is not surprising, given the varied methodologies reported across studies, the differences in the measurement of predictors, and the heterogeneous nature of the samples. Thus, any attempts to interpret the overall average ES may be misleading, and hence a further exploration is required in identifying which of the factors is accounting for the effect.
A closer examination of the individual age groups examined across all predictors revealed an ES for family factors measured during early childhood (age range = birth to six years) was .13 (CI = .07-.18), which was significant ([Z.sub.c] = 4.59, p<.001). An ES of .13, however, suggests that family factors measured in early childhood are a weak predictor of adult criminality. While the ES for family factors measured during mid-childhood was modestly high at .30 (CI = -.04-.65), this effect only approached significance ([Z.sub.c] = 1.73, p<.08). On the other hand, the ES for family factors measured in adolescence (age range = 12 years and older) was .31 (CI = .13-.48), which was significant ([Z.sub.c] = 3.45, p < .01).

ANALYSIS BY FAMILY PREDICTOR

Static Risk

Family static-risk predictors include variables such as socio-economic status, mother's age at birth of child, birth and delivery complications, and parental criminal history. Regardless of the age groups at which the static risk predictors were measured (i.e., early childhood, mid-childhood, or adolescence), the overall ES was .15, which was significant (CI=.05-.26, [Z.sub.c] = 2.79, p<.01). An ES of .15, however, is small and, at least for the studies reviewed here, must be interpreted with caution. Static risk factors such as parental criminality, however, have been shown to be significant predictors of criminal acts in some studies (e.g., Farrington 1989), but this finding is not completely consistent across the literature (see Moffit 1987). The ES values for the three age groups (early childhood, mid-childhood, and adolescence) were not significant (ail p > .1). However, because of the heterogeneity of the methodologies, measures, and outcomes reported in the various studies, an examination for the individual factors is considered more reliable in reflecting the prediction of adult criminality. These areas included parental mental health, parent management, family structure, and adverse family environment.

Dynamic Risk

In terms of dynamic family risk, parent management that tends to be coercive, inconsistent, or lacking in supervision during mid-childhood emerged as a particularly strong predictor, with ES of .41 (CI = .17-.66; Zc = 3.30, p <.001). Family structure variables such as whether a child was involved in the child welfare system and marital status of the parents, regardless of the age groups, was significant, with an overall ES of .48 (CI = .17-.80; [Z.sub.c] = 2.98, p<.01). An ES of this magnitude is notable and suggests that family structure variables are important predictors of adult crime. Strikingly, the results of the family structure variables measured in adolescence were of particular importance (e.g., child welfare involvement, parental separation, marital status). The ES for these variables measured in adolescence was .67 (CI = .19-.15; [Z.sub.c] = 2.71, p<.01).

Adverse family environment factors (e.g., family violence) were used as predictors of adult crime, and, regardless of the age groups at which the adverse family environment predictors were measured, the overall ES was .23 (CI = .08-.38; [Z.sub.c] = 2.99,

170

p<.001). Factors such as witnessing family violence and child maltreatment are modest predictors of adult crime. One would have expected, however, that the ES for factors such as child maltreatment would be stronger, given the established literature on child maltreatment and adult crime (Smith and Thornberry 1995). However, given the heterogeneous nature of the studies examining adverse family environments, and the varied definitions of family violence, the smaller ES may not be surprising.

DISCUSSION

Meta-analysis has assisted the field of criminal justice in developing models of risk assessment. Such assessment strategies have supported efforts in refining program planning and service delivery. The field of developmental criminology in criminal justice has a particularly important role to play in this context as it reflects, within a developmental framework, those issues that children and youth contend with that can place them at ongoing risk for antisocial outcomes. This review employed longitudinal and prospective studies within a meta-analytic framework in examining predictors that relate to being involved in the adult criminal justice system. The results are interpreted against meta-analyses that employ cross-sectional studies, predictors in the context of developmental differences, child versus family predictors, and finally the relevance of the current findings to service utilization in prevention.

RELEVANCE TO CROSS-SECTIONAL PREDICTORS OF RISK

The following list of factors were identified as particularly strong predictors from the present analysis: behavioural difficulties including hyperactivity, aggression, and conduct disorder; emotional concerns including depression; family factors that include coercive, inconsistent parent management that also lacks supervision; marital status of the parents; and witnessing family violence and child maltreatment. From the summary provided by Borum (2000), predominant predictors from the cross-sectional literature that agree with the present findings include all factors noted from the present study. Hence, confidence should increase in appreciating the convergence of findings from the present longitudinal studies with previously reported cross-sectional results.

DEVELOPMENTAL DIFFERENCES

The major area of contribution from the present meta-analysis lies in furthering the understanding of developmental differences and risk. Again, Borum (2000) suggests that precision in the assessment of risk increases as our appreciation increases of the developmental context in which a risk factor occurs. To review, the goal of this analysis was to examine the pervasive impact of risk as it relates to involvement in the adult criminal justice system. Major findings that emerge emphasized that certain factors become increasingly stable as predictors with the increasing age of the child. In other words, measures taken in adolescence are stronger predictors than those identified when a child is younger. In addition, and consistent with developmental and social learning theory, systemic factors of risk proved to be stronger predictors relative to individual child predictors. Hence, the nature of parent management viewed as inconsistent, harsh, or punitive, along with a child's experience with violence in the home, both as a witness and as a victim, proved to be particularly strong family-based predictors. This too would be consistent with the numerous commentaries extending from Bronfenbrenner to Henggeler, who emphasize the importance of systemic variables in understanding childhood development generally and risk prediction in particular.

In addition, and as underscored by Andrews and Bonta (2007), understanding of risk prediction and assessment strongly supports the view that it is the combination of factors as well as the intensity of a specific risk factor that leads to the overall potency of prediction. Within a developmental framework, some speculation can be made about the experience of children who are challenged with risk at different developmental periods. For example, child-specific risk - including a variety of behavioural disorders in combination with being the recipient of harsh or inconsistent parenting and exposure and victimization of violence within the home that can co-occur or follow in a sequence of risk--can incrementally increase the accuracy of prediction. Studies that assist in this regard utilize a path analysis or hierarchical linear modelling to investigate the additive and sequential effects of risk exposure across developmental periods.

RELEVANCE TO SERVICE UTILIZATION

Risk prediction and assessment have assisted service planning in two ways. First, they have provided a context in which to consider the intensity of service. Based on risk-assessment models, the service paradigm supports the view that higher-risk cases will benefit from more intensive forms of service, with lower-risk cases benefiting from less-intensive service. Second, risk assessment has also served as the basis for the selection of and priority given to certain targets of service. Tolan (2001) suggests that, within a developmental-ecological framework, of which this meta-analysis is an example, service providers may increasingly be able to refine intervention decisions beyond the intensity and focused selection of treatment targets to move to decision making on the timeliness of intervention within a developmental framework.

LIMITATIONS AND FUTURE DIRECTIONS

The value and contribution of any meta-analysis depends upon the number and quality of the studies that are available. The present analysis was ambitious in restricting the selection of studies to reflect longitudinal prospective studies that track children and youth to at least their eighteenth birthday or age of entering the adult criminal justice system in the country of origin. To a great degree, the results confirm the consistency in identifying the risk factors that have also been identified in the cross-sectional literature. Where inconsistencies do occur, caution should be used in not interpreting the lack of evidence as undermining those findings based on the longitudinal literature.

This is an evolving database from which to draw, and this meta-analysis represents an early attempt to restrict the selection of studies to longitudinal studies only as the sole source for the meta-analysis. Although it is encouraging that 38 studies met our selection criteria, the scope of dependent and independent variables addressed in the literature presented some limitations in how we conducted our analyses. It would have been informative, for example, to focus on differences in effect sizes for important predictors across developmental stages, or between males and females. To focus a study on a single set of predictors such as substance abuse or depressive symptoms could provide the necessary details needed to inform clinical practice, interventions, and public policy. It would also be important to distinguish between self- and official reports, and to determine if significant differences in effect sizes exist for these different sources of data. However, given the relatively large number of dependent variables in the current literature base, limitations in how studies reported data pertaining to independent variables, and the comparatively small number of studies that fit our rigorous selection criteria, we were not able to carry out more detailed analyses. We hope that the limitations of our study can be addressed in future meta-analyses that will have access to a larger pool of research.

VIEWING YOUTH PREVENTION WITHIN A DEVELOPMENTAL FRAMEWORK

Recent work in the area of child and youth prevention has promoted a focus in two directions. The first examines the benefits of prevention relative to the costs of tracking the impact of certain outcomes that could have been prevented, had the services been in place. The work of the Washington State Institute for Public Policy (2004) characterizes its reviews of the effectiveness of prevention within this framework in two ways. First, risk in prevention promotes understanding about the impact of service, measuring the outcomes in relevant and useful terms. The second (which has captured the interest of policy makers and legislators in particular) is the importance of measuring the impact of service upon the costs of offering the service. In other words, when it comes to prevention in measuring the benefits of reducing offending in youth justice, how much community safety can be "purchased," factoring in the costs of service delivery?

The second focus in prevention, and the area where the current findings have the greatest relevance, lies in the increased emphasis given to viewing prevention within a social developmental framework. Dahlberg and Potter (2001) suggest that we can maximize the benefits of prevention by appreciating that risk factors will interact differentially at different developmental periods. Farrington and Welsh (2007) provided convincing evidence for the ability of service providers to intervene effectively when early risk factors are known. For example, in early childhood, family factors including coercive parenting and child maltreatment will play a more significant role than peer influence and substance use, which are among two of the more significance risk factors affecting adolescence. The relevance of this type of analysis, as suggested by Dahlberg and Potter, lies in "providing some indication of where to focus preventive efforts" (4). While some of the findings from the present study suggest that some predictors of risk are applicable across all age groupings such as behavioural indicators of aggression and an inability to focus attention, other risk factors are unique to specific developmental periods. Earlier indicators of risk that are developmentally sensitive reflect a child's reaction to systemic influences primarily within the family. Examples of these predictors for adult offending include early victimization through child maltreatment and the experience of vicarious trauma through family violence.

Specific to focusing prevention efforts to interrupt a trajectory that leads to involvement in the adult criminal justice system, a model that differentially focuses efforts at reducing risk would include the following:

* In early childhood a focus on factors related to violence in the family, either with a child being the victim of maltreatment or traumatized by violence between caregivers

* In middle childhood and adolescence an increasing focus on family-related risk such as supervision, the nature of parenting, and the impact of violence in the family

      While such possibilities for increasing prevention effectiveness await empirical outcomes, the current meta-analysis adds to our increasing confidence in the potential to use a developmental framework within which to plan such prevention.

Alan Leschied
The University of Western Ontario
Debbie Chiodo
Centre for Addiction and Mental Health
Elizabeth Nowicki and Susan Rodger
The University of Western Ontario

2

Wayward Youth, Super Predator: An Evolutionary Tale of Juvenile Delinquency from the 1950s to the Present

The New Breed of Juvenile Offender

Stephen Gluck

Author's Abstract

Juveniles in the 1950s were considered wayward kids, not "super predators," cruel young people who do not consider the consequences of their actions. Juvenile facilities kept young people busy with classes and recreational activities. Therapy and counseling became an important part of rehabilitation programs during the 1970s while special education programs were developed in the 1980s. Although crowding remains a problem in 1997, new adaptations and programs are continuously being developed.

A little human touch can go a long way toward improving the behavior of troubled youth. Or so believes Carl Oliver, the retired superintendent of a juvenile detention center just outside Washington, D.C.

Oliver tells the story of one youth under his care who, with some encouragement, became the institution's artist-in-residence.

Wayward Youth, super predator: An evolutionary tale of juvenile delinquency from the 1950s to the present (1997), by Stephen Gluck. Corrections Today, June 1997, v59 n3, p62 (4). Reprinted by permission.

176

According to Oliver, the boy had refused to pay attention in class, and was ordered to stay behind each day to make up for the time he had wasted. To alleviate his boredom, the boy doodled in his notebook. Oliver saw creativity in the drawings and encouraged him to continue. It wasn't long before the boy was commissioned to decorate the school's walls. He also stopped acting up in class and became a better student.

"Kids need recognition and new experiences," Oliver says. "Get them in a situation where there is understanding, and changes can take place."

Since the 1950s, many changes have taken place at juvenile detention centers. The cottage-type facilities from Oliver's time have given way to the more institutional-type settings common today. At the same time, the number of offenders, and the severity of their crimes, has increased.

THE NEW BREED

In the past, many of the juveniles in the system were not considered hardened criminals, but simply wayward youngsters who had strayed from the right path. Today, buzzwords such as "super predator" are used increasingly in the press and by politicians to describe the new type of youthful offender - ruthless young men and women who see crime as a rite of passage and who are unconcerned about the consequences of their actions.

Television news splatters images of heinous Crimes perpetrated by youthful offenders; and politicians, eager to look tough on crime, issue promises that they will cure America of this disease by severely cracking down on juvenile delinquency. Although the attacks win political points, not everyone is convinced of their merit. Juvenile justice experts say these attacks can be destructive.

"I thought it was deplorable the way the president and Mr. Dole went on about kids," says John Sheridan, speaking about Bill Clinton's and Bob Dole's tough talk on youth crime during last fall's election campaign. "That kind of talk and fear-mongering will make the situation worse."
Sheridan, a retired administrator of residential services in Concorde, N.H., says the media and politicians need to get their facts straight.

"No question there are more violent crimes today than there were 10 years ago," Sheridan says. But instead of blaming the youth, the media and politicians need to look at the root causes of juvenile delinquency - in particular, the breakdown of the family, child abuse, poverty and the ready availability of guns.

The atmosphere of blame has pressured justice departments in many states to ignore the causes and concentrate mainly on the crimes. As a result, more youths are being tried in criminal courts and sent to adult prisons. This is a departure from the way juveniles were handled in the past.

THE EARLY YEARS

According to Joanne Perkins, deputy director of the Juvenile Division of the Illinois Department of Corrections, the youths sent to institutions 40 years ago were mostly incorrigibles - runaways, prostitutes and children who could not be controlled by their parents. The facilities were low security and generally run by parents - a husband and wife who lived with and supervised children in the facility.

John Platt, an administrator of juvenile community services in Illinois, says the cottage environment of the older juvenile facilities attempted to make living arrangements seem as close as possible to life at home. The children lived dormitory-style in the cottages and meals were prepared and served by the cottage "mother." Maple Glen School, where Carl Oliver worked, had a setting similar to this.

Oliver says that at his facility in the 1950s, youths were kept busy with a full day at school and extensive recreational activities. A points program was in place to reward the students for positive behavior. The points were used to "buy" activities, such as camping and bicycling trips. Since many of the youths had never experienced these types of activities, the points program was a true incentive for them to do well in school. Oliver says the youngsters under his care were able to expand their horizons at the facility by participating in the program.

Along with the idea of positive reinforcement came a reluctance to administer severe punishment. In fact, any form of punishment was seen as a last resort. If a child got out of control, he would be locked in a cottage. Oliver says he insisted that children not be hit.

"Once you begin to escalate action, the whole thing gets worse and worse," Oliver says. "You must have an honest and fair approach to discipline."

He says many of the children who came to Maple Glen had social problems - they didn't receive enough attention from their parents or had problems in school. One of the functions of his institution was to instill confidence in the children through recognition of individual talents and abilities.

178

"Love and empathy must be engendered and worked into the systems" Oliver says.

With added confidence, many children improved their performance at school. In one instance, Oliver asked a boy why his schoolwork had improved so markedly. The boy answered that at the institution, he felt the staff cared about his progress.

To these children, "you're either a friend or a fraud," Oliver says.

COUNSELING COMPONENT

In the 1970s, status offenders no longer came under the jurisdiction of corrections, so adjustments had to be made in staffing and security requirements to deal with these changes. Staff became better trained and more in tune with the needs of the juveniles under their care. New correctional programs also were introduced to treat the youths. These changes, along with changes in state labor laws governing correctional workers, led to the demise of the Ma-and-Pa cottages.

New programs focused on treating the child as a whole person. Years ago, schooling was the main thrust of juvenile detention. Under programs introduced in the 1970s, education was still important, but it was not the only component of treatment. Emphasis was placed on therapy and counseling. Perkins says part of the rehabilitation program involved instilling into the juveniles values and ethics, as well as working on decision-making skills to teach right from wrong.

One program that was in use was called Guided Group Interaction. Juveniles were placed in small groups for counseling, schooling and other activities. Advocates thought this type of environment would allow guidance to take place through the groups.

According to Perkins, the best programs involved all the staff - teachers, doctors and counselors - working together to "deal with the whole kid." That meant not just looking at the youth's criminal activity, but at his or her strengths, talents, background and weaknesses as well.

As facilities received more youths who committed "adult" crimes, the public became concerned that juvenile correctional facilities in their communities posed a potential danger to their neighborhoods.

"The public did not want a kid who committed a crime to be able to walk into their homes," Perkins says.

To address public concern, the institutions were made more secure. Facilities were fenced, more security personnel were added and individual rooms were secured. Security also was a concern inside the facilities, and an improved ratio of staff to juveniles created a safer environment.

UNPRECEDENTED GROWTH

The 1980s saw growth in adult corrections. This, combined with decreases in budgets for youth corrections, led to cutbacks in programs for juveniles. Facilities incorporated the best of the old programs into newer, more cost-effective ones.

Special education programs were developed. By focusing on each youngster individually, correctional workers were able to create programs that best used the skills of each child. Special education workers also were hired to facilitate these new programs.

As the decade wore on, more youths were admitted to facilities, leading to crowding problems. In many cases, the number of staff stayed constant, while the number of juveniles increased. Crowding problems were a potential challenge to the ability of programs to run successfully. Many of the programs worked best in settings of between 25 and 50 people. Changes were made so that juveniles would still receive the appropriate counseling and education.

In Illinois, staff hours were changed so that activities could go on all day, Perkins recalled. Even school hours were extended to ensure that everyone had an opportunity to attend class.

TODAY'S CHALLENGES

Adaptations and new programs continue to be developed today. In particular, military-style boot camps have been introduced in recent years to drill discipline and coax self-worth into juveniles. Treatment programs that address the individuals' deficiencies, along with educational programs, go hand-in-hand with the military exercises.

While many in the juvenile justice field were at first opposed to boot camps, some are starting to see their benefits. Perkins says she had initial reservations about their value because she did not think it was beneficial to run youths down in order to raise them back up. But after visiting a few camps, she was satisfied that boot camps that promote growth without first stripping juveniles of their spirit can have a positive impact on young people's behavior. Many states are now looking to boot camps to alleviate some of the pressures on juvenile correctional facilities.

However, even with the alternatives to traditional juvenile institutions, crowding continues to be a problem. According to a fact sheet prepared by the National Center for Juvenile Justice (NCJJ), juvenile arrests between 1988 and 1992 increased by 11 percent. This increase put further pressure on the juvenile correctional system. Another troubling number is the increase in murder arrests - up 51 percent for juveniles. Here, the numbers meet the media hype.

Although the number of violent juveniles arrested in a given year is still quite small - NCJJ estimates put the figures at less than one-half of 1 percent of youth - the perception of the dangerous youth remains. This accounts for the pressure to punish juveniles for their crimes by waiving them to criminal courts.

Mary Ann Saar, who has worked in both adult and juvenile facilities in Maine, says the term "punishment" was rarely used in the past to refer to juveniles, but many states now have the term in their juvenile codes. "People have been looking for a silver-bullet answer to juvenile crime," Saar says. "The focus is more on locking them up than on treatment."

Saar, like John Sheridan, says the root causes of delinquency must be explored as a way to decrease the problem. "Kids grow up without parental models," Saar says. "How can we expect them to behave in a manner they have never been taught?"

Many experts in juvenile justice stress the need to work with families and communities to diffuse problems before they get out of hand. "Before we put all this money into jails, we must look at education and strengthening the family," says Mel Brown, executive director of the Montgomery County Community Supervision and Corrections Division in Texas.

According to Brown, just getting tough and locking juveniles up for long periods will not solve the problem. "When values are not being taught, when you have low self-concepts, you are going to get attention one way or another," Brown says.

And attention - from the press, politicians and the public - is what juvenile delinquents are getting. Many see "The Get Tough Approach" as the way to deal with young offenders. They want more jails built and tougher sentences enforced.

But many of those who work with juvenile delinquents want more emphasis put on treatment programs so that the interned youth have an opportunity to be rehabilitated. "If we send kids back out angrier than when they came in, then we have missed what we should have done," says Joanne Perkins.

During the past 40 years, correctional facilities have changed in structure, security and programming, both in response to juveniles and the environment of the time. Those who work in the industry do what they can to help those in their care, but realize that outside factors must be addressed to reduce delinquency.

Carl Oliver recounts the tale of a boy who so badly wanted to return to the facility after he was released that he stole a bike and rode back. These stories recounted tenfold over the years beg the question: Do juvenile facilities protect society from the youths under their care, or do they protect delinquent youths from society? Perhaps a bit of both, juvenile experts agree.

3

OJJDP Develops Strategy to Reduce Juvenile Violence

John J. Wilson

Author's Abstract

The Office of Juvenile Justice and Delinquency Prevention has developed the Comprehensive Strategy for Serious, Violent and Chronic Juvenile Offenders to reduce juvenile delinquency and violence. The program seeks to unite public and private efforts and resources nationwide in the effort to fight crime at its roots. The prevention and intervention components of the program are discussed, and the implementation strategy is presented.

Attorney General Janet Reno and the U.S. Justice Department's Office of Juvenile Justice and Delinquency Prevention (OJJDP) are calling for an unprecedented national commitment of public and private resources, energy and commitment to reducing juvenile violence and juvenile victimization in our nation. OJJDP's Comprehensive Strategy for Serious, Violent and Chronic Juvenile Offenders is the centerpiece of this effort.

OJJDP's strategy is a system-wide approach for dealing with serious, violent and chronic juvenile delinquency. It has two main components: prevention and intervention. Prevention and early intervention programs for first-time offenders are the most cost-effective strategies for deterring youths who are at risk of becoming serious, violent or chronic career criminals. The alternative--waiting until a juvenile must be incarcerated--is far too expensive: In its Dec. 13, 1993, issue, Business Week reported that the cost of

OJJDP develops strategies to reduce juvenile violence. Dept. of Justice, Office of juvenile justice and delinquency prevention: Stemming the Violence, by John J. Wilson. (1994). Corrections Today, August 1994, v. 56, no 5. P118 (4). Reprinted by permission.

incarcerating a juvenile is $20,000 to $30,000 per year, and imprisoning a 25-year-old for life costs $600,000 to $1 million.

PREVENTION COMPONENT

The strategy's prevention component calls on communities to systematically assess their delinquency problem in relation to known risk factors and to set up programs to counteract them.

What can communities and the juvenile justice system do to prevent at-risk youths from developing into career criminals? Juvenile justice agencies and programs are one piece of a larger picture involving many other local agencies and programs that work with at-risk youths and their families. Comprehensive approaches to delinquency prevention and intervention require collaborative efforts between the juvenile justice system and other service providers such as health, mental health, child welfare and education systems. Linking these service providers at the program level must be an important component of every community's comprehensive plan.

INTERVENTION COMPONENT

The strategy's intervention component is based on the recognition that an effective model for handling delinquent offenders must combine accountability and sanctions with increasingly intensive treatment and rehabilitation programs.

The intervention component establishes a range of graduated sanctions that features both immediate interventions and intermediate sanctions, including extensive use of nonresidential community-based programs. Intermediate sanctions use both nonresidential and residential programs, including intensive supervision programs for both repeat and first-time violent offenders.

Some serious, violent and chronic offenders need to be housed in secure detention and corrections programs to protect the community and ensure that they receive treatment in a structured environment. OJJDP believes small community-based facilities with a structured setting and intensive therapeutic environments offer the best possibility for success with these juveniles. All sectors of the community must take part in determining local needs and in planning and implementing programs to meet those needs by providing a continuum of care.

STRATEGY IMPLEMENTATION

Last year, OJJDP funded Graduated Sanctions projects in Allegheny County, Pa., and Washington, D.C. In fiscal year 1994, OJJDP will award grants to two new jurisdictions under a competition announced in June. OJJDP also is compiling information on a wide variety of effective delinquency prevention programs and preparing a blueprint to guide communities in assessing their juvenile justice system and planning new programs to better respond to juveniles' needs.

One of the primary objectives of OJJDP's strategy is to improve the administration and management of the juvenile justice system. OJJDP has identified 10 major goals for juvenile justice, each of which has implications for juvenile detention and corrections.

Delinquency prevention must be a community priority. Advanced delinquency prevention is patterned after successful efforts in the health arena. University of Washington researchers David Hawkins and Richard Catalano have developed a risk-focused prevention strategy that actively involves community leaders in assessing the range of local risk factors and identifying the most prevalent ones.

The community then selects specific program models that address these risk factors and prevent delinquent behavior. It is critical that juvenile justice system officials, including those in the detention and corrections fields, be actively involved in these community efforts.

Due process and quality legal representation for juveniles must be addressed. Ensuring the due process rights of juveniles and providing them with competent legal counsel is in the best interests of the youths and the justice system. Juvenile court judges and corrections officials can in turn use due process procedures to hold service providers accountable and to measure program performance.

Disproportionate confinement of minority youths must be eliminated. Disproportionate representation of minorities in secure juvenile facilities must be eradicated. From 1987 to 1991, the percentage of minority juveniles securely detained or confined increased from 53 percent to 63 percent. OJJDP has funded a five-state pilot program in Arizona, Florida, Iowa, North Carolina and Oregon to demonstrate techniques for reducing the disproportionate detention and confinement of minority youths. Technical assistance will be provided to other states so they can use the knowledge gained from this program.

Detention facility and training school populations must be decreased to their design capacity. An OJJDP study funded by Abt Associates found that more than 75 percent of the confined juvenile population is housed in facilities that violate one or more standards related to living space. Further, crowding is associated with higher rates of institutional violence, suicidal behavior and a greater reliance on the use of short-term isolation.

Tools are available to help correct this problem. For example, risk-assessment instruments classify juveniles into groups based on objective criteria related to the seriousness of the delinquent act, the potential risk for reoffending and the risk to public safety. These assessments can be used to identify lower risk youths who can be moved to community-based or alternative programs and services to relieve crowding.

Identification of treatment needs must be improved. Advanced techniques are available to assist juvenile justice professionals in assessing their clients' treatment needs. Needs-assessment technology, which helps officials allocate and target scarce resources more effectively and efficiently, has improved greatly over the past few years.

The costs associated with juvenile corrections must be reduced. The annual cost of confining juveniles in public facilities alone exceeds $2 billion. Use of OJJDP's strategy, coupled with the use of sophisticated risk assessments to identify juveniles who do not require secure confinement and who can be safely treated in community-based programs, would result in substantial savings nationwide.

A range of program options must be available to meet the needs of each juvenile in the system. Juvenile justice professionals must have access to a range of treatment options that addresses the array of cross-disciplinary problems identified by the needs assessment. Missouri has established an innovative statewide system of pooling funds in multiple service areas so that treatment resources follow the juvenile, rather than vice versa. Virginia also is experimenting with pooled resources on a smaller scale.

The use of alternatives to incarceration for nonviolent accused and adjudicated offenders must be increased. Most nonviolent offenders, including minor offenders, first-time serious offenders, repeat property offenders and drug-involved juveniles, can be rehabilitated successfully and controlled without adjudication and confinement. Intermediate sanctions are appropriate for many adjudicated youths. A combination of nonresidential and residential sanctions should be used.

Conditions of confinement must be improved. The Abt study revealed serious deficiencies in the management and operation of juvenile detention and correctional facilities, many of which could be ameliorated at a reasonable cost. Abt researchers identified three major problems.

First, they reported that several areas within juvenile facilities have substantial and widespread problems, including living spaces, health care, security and monitoring of suicidal behavior. The researchers also found that high levels of conformance to nationally recognized standards do not necessarily result in improved conditions of confinement because most standards only require that policies and procedures be in place. Performance standards are needed to monitor service delivery and the quality of life for confined juveniles. Finally, the Abt study found widespread deficiencies across facilities and facility types. Thus, the study concluded, broad-based improvement efforts are needed.

Effective aftercare programs must be developed. Aftercare is typically the weakest link in the continuum of care. To address this problem, OJJDP has helped develop an intensive after-care program model for high-risk juveniles that will assist jurisdictions in building an effective aftercare system. Officials in eight states have been trained in the administration of the program, and OJJDP will implement a statewide intensive aftercare program in at least four of these states in fiscal year 1994.

ACA PROJECTS

ACA and OJJDP are currently collaborating on several projects. With its technical assistance and training grant, ACA sponsored day treatment conferences in Kentucky in 1993 and in Florida in 1994. Both conferences were highly successful. ACA focused on day treatment programs because they have important implications for relieving crowding and will be addressed in OJJDP's conditions of confinement study.

ACA also is developing a training curriculum in cultural differences for law enforcement and juvenile justice officials. This project will help prevent disparate treatment of minority youths by the juvenile justice system while enhancing the safety and effectiveness of juvenile justice professionals working in minority communities.

Another ACA project involves testing juvenile detainees for illegal drug use. ACA is developing model drug testing programs for juveniles in detention facilities and has produced a manual to help guide the creation of drug testing policies and procedures and to assist with training.

ACA's law-related education in juvenile justice settings program was funded in October 1993 as part of a collaborative effort between ACA, the Juvenile Justice Trainers Association and the New York Division of Youth. In the coming months, several demonstration sites will incorporate law-related education methods and curricula into daily programming.

For more than a century, ACA has been actively involved in developing a national correctional philosophy; designing and implementing standards for correctional services and methods for measuring compliance; and providing publications, training and technical assistance to professionals in the field. The ACA Executive Committee, Board of Governors, and staff are to be commended for their many accomplishments.

OJJDP believes much more can be done to improve juvenile corrections and detention in the United States. We must remember that juvenile offenders are adolescents with the potential to change their lives with the appropriate intervention. If we do not adopt strategies to address juvenile violence, these children will become tomorrow's adult inmates--draining more and more of society's resources.

John J. Wilson is acting administrator of the Office of Juvenile Justice and Delinquency Prevention, U.S. Department of Justice.

4

Why We Can't Wait: The Juvenile Court in the New Millennium

Glenda Hatchett

Abstract

The juvenile justice system is in turmoil, lacking foresight and preventive measures needed for lasting reform. Resources should no longer be given to programs that do not have clear commitment to children and families. Too many people draw salaries in the name of children without helping them. Recidivism rates are higher among juveniles tried in adult court and reactionary politics have controlled the destiny of the US. There are too many minority youths in the juvenile and criminal justice systems because of systematic racism, classism and discrimination in adjudication of juvenile cases.

In 1963, Dr. Martin Luther King Jr. sat in a cramped Birmingham jail composing a letter to his fellow Alabama clergymen. With great effort, Dr. King tried to explain how "wait almost always means never," and why "direct action ... is never `well-timed' in the view of those who have not suffered unduly." It is with that same sense of "unavoidable impatience" and urgency for change that I have come to view the current juvenile justice system's focus on punitive justice and its inadequate commitment to systemic intervention and prevention. In 1996, more than 15,000 children came through the Fulton County Juvenile Court in Atlanta, Georgia, alone.

This country has responded to juvenile crime by creating "get tough" and "three strikes" legislation that focuses on children

Why we can't wait: The juvenile court in the new millennium. (Special Issue: NCCD 90th Anniversary), by Glenda Hatchett. Crime and delinquency, January 1998, v44 n1 p. 83(6). Reprinted by permission.

who have already penetrated the system so deeply that it has become easy for people to no longer claim them as their own. The juvenile court has a unique opportunity to divert children from crime and delinquency and to reframe the discussion so that we are focused on what we do before strike one. In the new millennium, the juvenile court must focus on early intervention and prevention-based programming to effectively address the needs of America's children. It is time that we take "direct action" on their behalf. We only get one chance to get it right for this generation of children while they are still our children, and surely that is why we can't wait.

The 100-year anniversary of the juvenile court is being ushered in with debates about the effectiveness of this system that has been created to deal with juvenile offenders. There is little argument that the current juvenile justice system is indeed in turmoil and lacks the foresight and preventive measures required for lasting reform. We do little good rehashing the problems we all know exist. I submit that the debate must center on where we must go from here and how to get there.

Juvenile courts across the nation are dealing with an escalating number of children, but these courts have deteriorated due to the lack of creative visions, adequate funding, and stagnating policies. The answer is not reactionary laws or the dismantling of the system as a whole. We cannot afford to abandon the traditional premise of the juvenile justice system, which was created specifically to provide individualized treatment and services for troubled children. Instead, we must be willing to abandon outmoded, outdated, and archaic practices we know do not work.

When I think of what reforms must be made in the juvenile justice system of the new millennium, I am reminded of David. David came before me my first year on the bench. He was 11 and notorious. He had stolen more cars than I have owned in my lifetime, and everyone in the juvenile court knew him. I thought, "How hard could it be to get your hands on an 11-year-old child and turn his life around?" I wanted David to spend Christmas at home instead of the detention center he so often frequented, so I gave him a long lecture about promises. I told him as my father told me, and as I tell my sons, that your word is your bond. Promises are made to be kept. That day David made a promise to me that he would not get into any more trouble. We sealed it with a handshake, and I let him go. Before the Christmas holidays were over, David stood before me again on more serious charges. I remember watching him being led away and wondering why he did not keep his promise. David, like many children who have come before me since him, had been involved with governmental agencies all of his young life. He was born to an alcoholic mother and had been brutally beaten every day that he could remember. At 6 years old, an uncle came promising a safe haven but instead raped and sodomized the child repeatedly. David had been in and out of more institutions than he could remember, and I wondered why David cannot keep a promise? He had never known anyone in his life to keep a promise to him.

Had the proper intervention and prevention programs been in place, I believe that the David who stood before me that day would not have been there. We must keep in mind that children like David are first victims, products of years of broken American promises. In the new millennium, we cannot afford to have any more Davids become casualties of our unwillingness or our inability to effectively intervene early in a child's life.

It must be implicit in our efforts to save children's lives that effective intervention means that there has got to be zero tolerance for poverty pimps and "broken promises programs." Poverty pimps are more concerned about funding cycles and administrative overhead than programmatic integrity. Time, money, and resources cannot continue to be allocated to agencies, people, or programs that have not demonstrated a clear commitment to children and families. There are too many people on payrolls who are doing nothing but drawing breath and salaries in the name of our children. We must be willing to call it as we see it. The juvenile justice system has become an intensive care unit for our nation's children, and in their eyes I see all that ails America: poverty, homelessness, poor education, and more. We must take "direct action" for our children. The challenge before us is to move from the rhetoric to the reality of what we are going to do to save their lives and our collective futures.

We have allowed reactionary politics to control the destiny of our country. Hoping to be safe from the wrath of children who have been ignored and neglected from birth, states are trying children as adults in escalating numbers. There will always be children who, due to the heinous nature of their crimes, must be tried and treated as adults. That is the reality of the situation, but that decision is better made by juvenile court judges on a case-by-case basis. Waiver and transfer laws are seen as a quick fix for crime in America, but they are no panacea for our problems. Many of the studies show that the recidivism rates are much higher among juveniles tried in adult court. If we are truly committed to deterring children from crime, then how can this be our solution for change? The hallmark of the juvenile court is individualized treatment. We gain greater control of our communities and children when we set clear expectations and examples for their future. The relief from crime promised by these haphazardly created laws is not forthcoming. When we place children in institutions where they often sit for months, accused but not convicted, we lose a window of opportunity to turn their lives around. We do nothing more than create better criminals. These children inevitably reenter society no better equipped to be productive citizens than when they were first detained. Automatically trying juveniles as adults gives up on them before we have made any real effort to show them a better way.

Furthermore, the criminal and juvenile justice systems are not immune from the "isms" that plague most institutions of America. Systematic racism, classism, and discrimination in the adjudication of juvenile cases have led to the overrepresentation of minority youths in the juvenile and criminal justice systems. Black youths only make up 15% of all young people in this nation, but they occupy 65% of all bed space in detention facilities. Forty-nine percent of all juveniles arrested for violent crime are Black. Fifty-two percent of all children who are transferred to stand trial as adults are Black children. Native American youths make up 60% of the children prosecuted in the adult federal system. Surely, we must find a better way to keep our communities safe and rehabilitate our children where the scales of justice will not be so unbalanced.

I am well aware that every child cannot be helped in the same manner. There are children who need to be dealt with in restrictive custody for the safety of the community as well as their own. I make no excuse for abominable behavior. The effect of societal ills on children is not an excuse, but we must acknowledge that it is a root cause of the behavior we seek to modify. Prevention and intervention are not mutually exclusive from more punitive measures, but we can make no lasting difference in the number of children in the system without equal attention being paid to both. There must be a continuum of options for dealing with children who commit delinquent acts because we cannot cure what we do not understand. We cannot continue to warehouse children in detention centers and jails and believe that the nation's juvenile crime problem will be solved. Juvenile courts must provide alternative and diverse, yet efficient and effective, processing of juvenile and family matters.

All too often the issue of drug abuse has been at the core of children's issues. With the introduction of crack cocaine into American communities, more children have entered the juvenile justice system than ever before. I've seen a baby born addicted to crack who screamed incessantly from unidentified pains. I've seen a 12-year-old dealer who sold drugs on the corner to support a family of four. I've seen a 5-year-old boy prostituted by his own mother in exchange for cocaine. Sadly, drug addiction is oftentimes more powerful than family ties. The 1990s saw a shift in this country's drug policies that provided stiffer penalties for adults in the drug industry. Unfortunately, those who prey on the weak found that our children are dispensable and began to use them as drug carriers more frequently than in the past. Nationwide there are thousands of children born to addicted parents and/or involved in drug trafficking. Their lives have been shattered by the scourge of drugs. Their lives belong to the so-called lost generation for whom too many in our society have already written a eulogy, but we must not concede defeat in the battle for the futures of our young and unborn. We must reclaim our children and proclaim our unwillingness to wait on their predicted collective demise.

The courts must intervene to ensure that effective substance abuse treatment and education for children and their families are available. Serious substance abuse at any age is not apt to be remedied without the benefit of treatment and long-term rehabilitation services. Community-based substance abuse programs must be developed and connected with the juvenile court to provide wraparound services that attack the very foundation of the problem in the community. Seventy-four percent of all abuse and neglect cases that were heard in my court in 1996 involved substance abuse issues. America must respond to the drug epidemic at home with the same vigor, determination, resources, and singleness of purpose that have been marshaled to ostensibly liberate people halfway around the world. Until we deal with this epidemic head on, this country will continue to tread water on many critical issues.

The view from the bench is sometimes awfully bleak, but I am not without hope. With all of the statistics and information disseminated regarding policies, procedures, and programs, we lose sight of what is making a difference in our communities. Prevention works. I believe that the implementation of programs that are designed to divert children from the juvenile justice system will make a profound difference in the numbers of children who repeatedly come before the court. These programs must be comprehensive, culturally sensitive, child centered, and family focused. A program of early intervention must reach children at their first involvement with any government agency. It is at this point that certain "at-risk" factors need to be identified. Many children face multiple risk factors, such as teenage pregnancy, truancy, incorrigible behavior, running away from home, and economic, emotional, and physical deprivation. It is essential that the juvenile court be equipped with the necessary resources to address all of a child's needs.

A new paradigm must be devised for providing services to children and their families. We can no longer do so in a vacuum. To that end, a coordination and collaboration of the court with the proper community-based resources is imperative. Programs such as the Caring Communities Solving Problems Program (CCSP) demonstrate the necessity of community ownership in the successful restoration of families. CCSP concentrates on youths ages 13 to 17 who become involved with the Fulton County Juvenile Justice System. The success of this program is due to its comprehensive curriculum designed to address the risk factors of delinquency through the innovative use of adult and peer facilitators, as well as an intergenerational approach to problem solving. Children and their families are ordered by the court to attend classes on violence prevention, parenting skills, and drug and alcohol education. The holistic approach that CCSP uses allows the entire family to participate and become involved in the intervention and prevention process.

By evaluating indicators of delinquent behavior, comprehensive intervention and prevention programs can be created. Afterschool programming that engages children's minds and encourages school attendance can effectively reduce some of the risk factors children face. Of those aforementioned indicators, truancy is the number one predictor among boys of future criminal activity and the number two predictor among girls. Intervention and prevention programs that address the issues of truancy and provide afterschool activities should be at the core of any prevention program. One student drops out of school every 9 seconds. Most cases of juvenile crime, teenage pregnancy, and juvenile drug activity occur when children should be in school or during the few hours after school has been dismissed. These key hours are where we can make a difference.

In Atlanta, we have developed the Truancy Intervention Project (TIP), a wonderful partnership between the Fulton County Juvenile Court and the Atlanta Bar Foundation. The project provides volunteer attorneys and nonattorney partners to children whose truancy is their first encounter with the juvenile court. In recognition of the urgency of intervention, specific court resources and procedures for expedited case processing are in place. The juvenile court has access to the school system's automated attendance records to aid in allowing specially trained probation staff to monitor a child's attendance in school. The probation officers may also contact the schools through an innovative teleconferencing unit supplied by BellSouth. Since the program's inception, more than 500 youths have been served. Fifty-eight percent of the children have never had a subsequent court charge after their involvement with TIP, and less than 2% were committed to the Department of Children and Youth Services for subsequent delinquent behavior. Undereducation is the cause of many issues our children face. We must fight ignorance as if our lives depend on it, because they do.

It is awfully dark in America, and our children stand before us as future torchbearers. Many desire to illuminate the darkness, but they are not always able. Every day children are born fighting for life--too much of their precious blood flows in our streets. I suggest that it is incumbent on us to rekindle our own embers of hope, and then be willing to pass it on. Dr. Maya Angelou says, "We must bind ourselves to one another. We must: embrace our lowliest; keep company with our loneliest; educate our illiterate; feed our starving; and clothe our ragged. We must do all good things knowing that we are more than our brothers', sisters' [and children's] keepers. We are our brothers, sisters, [and our children]."

Juvenile courts can no longer stand as edifices of broken dreams and promises. Juvenile courts of the new millennium must be resource centers of tomorrow whose doors do not close at 5:00 p.m. Understand that the survival of children is not the juvenile court's problem in isolation. Communities must come together in the name of what is right. What is just is rarely easy, but if we do not do the collective work now, we will pay the collective price later. Paul Robeson once said, "The battlefront is everywhere, and there is no sheltered rear." I stand firmly on the principle that we can no longer run for cover behind Draconian measures or simply count casualties in this battle to save our children. Every 13 seconds a child is reported abused or neglected. Every 12 seconds a child drops out of school. Every 53 minutes a child dies from poverty. Every 3 hours a child is murdered. The battlefront is truly everywhere, and there is no sheltered rear.

Glenda Hatchett is Chief Judge of the Fulton County Juvenile Court in Atlanta, Georgia. Special thanks are given Deirdre Stephens and Jules Junker for their technical assistance.